Big Think Strategy

Big Think Strategy

How to Leverage Bold Ideas and Leave Small Thinking Behind

Bernd H. Schmitt

Harvard Business School Press • Boston, Massachusetts

No part of this publication may be reproduced, stored in or introduced into
a retrieval system, or transmitted, in any form, or by any means (electronic,
mechanical, photocopying, recording, or otherwise), without the prior
permission of the publisher. Requests for permission should be directed to
permissions@hbsp.harvard.edu, or mailed to Permissions, Harvard Business
School Publishing, 60 Harvard Way, Boston, Massachusetts 02163.

Library of Congress Cataloging-in-Publication Data
Schmitt, Bernd.
    Big think strategy : how to leverage bold ideas and leave small thinking
behind / Bernd H. Schmitt.
        p.   cm.
    Includes bibliographical references and index.
    ISBN-13: 978-1-4221-0321-0 (hardcover : alk. paper)
    ISBN-10: 1-4221-0321-8
    1. Creative ability in business. 2. Strategic planning. 3. Success in business.
 4. Organizational effectiveness. I. Title.
    HD53.S3596 2007
    658.4'012—dc22

                                                                2007021449

The paper used in this publication meets the requirements of the American
National Standard for Permanence of Paper for Publications and Documents
in Libraries and Archives Z39.48-1992.

To my little "Big Thinky Head,"

Thomas Fujii Schmitt,

seven years old

Contents

Acknowledgments   ix

1

Big Think and
the Trojan Horse

1

2

Sourcing Ideas

Steaks and Sacred Cows

25

3

Evaluating Ideas

How to Dig for the Gems

59

4

Turning Ideas into Strategy

What Would Mahler Do?

83

5

Executing Big Think

How to Pull the Ship over the Mountain

105

6

Leading Big Think

Guts, Passion—or Just a Robot?

121

7

Sustaining Big Think

From Sisyphus to Odysseus

139

Epilogue

161

Notes   165

Index   169

About Schmitt   179

Acknowledgments

Business leaders need creative and bold strategies to compete. Most strategy books, however, present familiar tools for analysis and planning that will never result in bold ideas that change markets.

Big Think Strategy is different. I will show you how to source bold and creative ideas, evaluate them, turn them into a strategy, and execute them. Moreover, you will see how to lead and build organizational structures that sustain what I call "Big Think."

This book is based on years of project work with companies globally. I have advised companies in consumer packaged goods, automotive, electronics, software, financial services, pharmaceuticals, beauty and cosmetics, hospitality, media, telecommunications, and the arts. At Columbia Business School, I teach a course on corporate creativity that won the school's "Innovation in the Classroom" award and a new project-based master class on market innovation. In my corporate seminars and workshops, I have tested the idea-sourcing, evaluation, and strategy tools presented in this book. I thank my students and clients for inspiring me to write this book.

I also would like to thank the many executives and experts who spoke with me about their projects and gave me written permission to quote them. All of the direct quotes in this book are original, based on these conversations and interviews (unless otherwise noted).

Several people helped me in the course of preparing the manuscript. Former Columbia students Aparna Swarts Mukherjee and Jenny Strasburg, who now work for the *Wall Street Journal* and Bloomberg, respectively, researched and drafted cases for me and interviewed several executives. Anna Peterson and Karen Vrotsos edited and proofread the manuscript. Jessica Wong, Garrett McDonough, and Dina Shapiro read the manuscript and secured rights. Several people read parts of the book, including my Columbia colleague Professor Asim Ansari and UCLA Professor Sanjay Sood. Another Columbia colleague, Professor Don Lehmann, along with Professor Dominique Hanssens of the Marketing Science Institute, gave me the opportunity to present my ideas and get feedback from executives and colleagues at their 2006 CMO Summit. April Cao, a former student and successful fashion entrepreneur in China, helped me greatly with the Trojan Horse project, and is using the book as a testing ground for some of her own projects, such as building global fashion brands.

I would not have been able to complete this book without the dedicated help of David Rogers and Nick Peterson. Both have worked with me for years at the Center on Global Brand Leadership at Columbia Business School. They researched and wrote cases for me, rewrote entire sections of the book, and gave me feedback in many-hours-long sessions. David also served as a sounding board for key book concepts, and Nick secured the rights for exhibits and photo images. You will meet both of them in this book in other roles: David is an accomplished composer and musician, and Nick, who grew up on a farm in Minnesota, showed me the connection between ideas and manure (as you will see in chapter 3).

My editor, Kirsten Sandberg, was a pleasure to work with. She challenged me to bring out my real personality with this book, in a way she felt my previous editors had not dared to do. "Be bold!" she advised me numerous times, "Schmitt it up!"

One way I decided to "Schmitt up" the book was to find inspiration not only in creative business practices of today, but also in the story of the Trojan Horse, in Mahler's symphonies, and in the movie *Fitzcarraldo*. Another part is breaking up the typical trade book writing style with personal stories here and there. You will learn about some of my personal tastes and preferences: I like a good steak, adore classical music (especially of German origin), and appreciate a good haircut. The book includes several episodes from my business travels, but in a narrative style inspired by recent movies like *Pulp Fiction, Traffic, Syriana,* or *Babel* that scramble time frames. I hope this creative license inspires you to take a creative spirit in your own work.

—Bernd H. Schmitt
New York City, July 2007

-1-

Big Think
and the
Trojan Horse

GENEVA, SWITZERLAND

I am in the front seat of the taxi. In the backseat: two
partners of a certain world-famous consulting firm that
advises clients on strategy. We are heading to the airport
after several days of intense work on one of their projects.

"We really have a tough time thinking big," the conversation starts.

"We have great analytic tools," the senior partner
explains. "If you give us a problem, some market data,
a map of your supply chain, whatever, we can dig in
better than anyone and tell you how to optimize your
current operations. But sometimes clients want something
completely different. Sometimes they give us a blank

slate and ask for bold new ideas. That's when we get really uncomfortable."

I have heard this many times, not only from consultants. Business leaders tell me that they want to think big. They know their organization's growth—and in some cases, its survival—depends on big ideas. Every success story they read or hear about involves a company led by bold thinking that has changed the marketplace to create new opportunity and new value. Interspersed are stories of once-great companies—Kodak, Xerox, Levi Strauss, AOL—that fell into painful and seemingly irreversible decline.

"They want a Trojan horse," I respond. They look at me confused. "Remember the Greeks, Odysseus and Agamemnon? Agamemnon led the greatest army of the ancient world, but for ten long years, he was unable to pierce the defenses of Troy's walled city. Along came Odysseus with the idea of offering the Trojans this giant wooden horse, ostensibly as a peace offering, but actually concealing Greek warriors inside the horse's hollow belly. The Trojans brought the horse inside their own walls. The Greek soldiers sneaked out, threw open the city gates, overwhelmed the city, and won the war overnight. That's Big Think."

They agree, "Great metaphor!"

I continue, "For me, the lesson of the Trojan horse for business is simple. Business leaders must free themselves of strategic planning processes that yield incremental results. They must take a truly creative approach to strategy development and execution."

**Bust of
Odysseus**

We reach the airport. As I gather my luggage from the trunk, the junior partner asks, "Don't you have some methodologies and tools that we can use, sort of plug into our projects, and then a big strategy just pops out?"

Big Think Versus Small Think

The chief executives, department heads, and entrepreneurs with whom I speak all say they need big and bold strategies to compete. They tell me they want to think out of the box, develop disruptive strategies, and execute in bold strokes that shake up markets.

So, the leaders all want to think big. Why don't they?

Because their organizations are trapped in a mode of small thinking that kills creativity right from the start. This kind of "Small Think" is characterized by inertia and resistance, narrow-mindedness, and risk aversion that stifle true innovation. Small Think is built into the siloed structure of most companies: manufacturing, marketing, sales, finance, human resources, service, and research and development. These silos operate independently and view each other as rivals not only for internal resources but also for talent and customers. From the tops of their functional silos, managers see only a narrow slice of the business and their short-term potential within it.

Small Think is sticking with the status quo and the same old procedures, planning tools, strategy maps, and research reports, even when they fail to produce bold ideas. Small Think is being held hostage to the next quarterly earnings report. Small Think is reactive and incremental.

Why does Small Think dominate strategic planning in so many organizations?

Small Think is known territory. Small Think is what managers get paid to do. Why stick your neck out when you do not know whether a new idea will actually work and whether you will get internal support to try it? Managers are rarely blamed for doing again and again what they have done in the past. If a brand, or a business unit, or an entire company must make a new move, the leader's safest choice is always the most certified, market-tested direction that dozens of other companies have no doubt already taken.

Small Think is easy. Those who pursue a bold new idea (especially for longer than a fiscal year) often get no reward or recognition because the company's incentive system is set up for predictable, short-term (even quarterly) results. Obviously, this kind of status quo is hazardous to the long-term health of any organization. Executives at every level seem to realize the disconnect between such standard Small Think procedures as annual budgeting and performance appraisals and the big thinking needed to achieve growth in a changing environment.

Big Think differs considerably from Small Think. (See table 1-1.) Big Think is a creative and visionary thinking and leadership style that leverages bold ideas and actions. Big Think organizations are integrated around a few core ideas that produce lasting impact.

Where Small Think deals with the known, the pretested, and the prechewed, Big Think faces challenges creatively, reasoning about them from new angles and generating innovative ideas and actions to solve them. Big Think does not just occur in the head. It involves action: managing people and teams, and driving organizational change. It is not simply creating something new; it is behaving differently.

Big Think is a style of thinking and leading. It is not something you get to by just collecting all the usual reams of business data, checking off your management boxes, and following a

FIGURE 1-1

Big Think versus Small Think

SMALL THINK		**BIG THINK**
Inertia and resistance	→	**Creativity and change**
Narrow-mindedness	→	**Visionary leadership**
Risk aversion	→	**Bold ideas and actions**
Silo mentality	→	**Integration across core ideas**
Short-term focus	→	**Lasting impact**

flowchart for decision making. Big Think has its own more creative methodologies and tools for idea sourcing, evaluation, strategy development, and execution. Big Think brings creative processes into strategic planning. Big Think is not just about "brainstorming." Big Think does not yield pie-in-the-sky ideas but creates detailed strategic plans that capitalize on real-world opportunities.

Where Small Think is compartmentalized into silos, Big Think rallies the whole organization around a few core ideas. Big Think aims for lasting impact. It creates new business models, disruptive technologies, and products and services that either change consumer behavior or accommodate an already changing behavior. Big Think alters the nature of competition. Once it is implemented, a particular industry is no longer the same. There is no going back.

Big Think transforms consumer expectations, preferences, and experiences. It changes how we shop and buy, and live and work. Since Starbucks, we can hang out in a "third space" that is neither home nor office but superior to other coffee shops. Since Ikea, we can easily shop for and assemble our furniture. Since Google, we can actually seek, find, and consume the sought-after information—and discover more that interests us.

Big Think and Business Success

Finding business examples of Big Think is not difficult. Every recent iconic business success belongs to visionaries who used big thinking to transform not just their company but the marketplace. You know them well.

The iPod did not succeed simply as a product—it transformed the music industry; revived its parent company, Apple Inc.; and changed how consumers organize, customize, and manage their music experience. In 2001, the music industry was trapped in inertia, narrow-mindedness, and risk aversion: the entire industry engaged in a self-destructive fight over digital rights, bickering endlessly about formats while its future revenue stream, the Napster generation, was learning to love digital music as a freebie. As an industry outsider, Steve Jobs could envision a device that combined the portability of an MP3 player, the organizing principle and service of a Napster, and the storage, programmability, and user-friendliness of an Apple computer. The iPod, with its seamless design, single-handedly created a mass market for MP3 players. With Apple's iTunes online music store, Jobs broke the deadlock over digital music distribution, coaxing the major record labels to offer their music for sale online. By 2006, Apple held a 74 percent U.S. market share in digital music players and was selling one hundred iPods a minute, many of them in the newly created Apple Stores. The iTunes online store dominated the music download market, selling over a billion songs in its first three years. With the launch of the iPhone, Apple continues its Big Think leadership in mobile electronics.

Whole Foods Market transformed the supermarket industry in the United States. For decades, supermarkets had competed by selling mediocre food at the lowest price. Profit margins were dwindling, labor troubles were frequent, and "double coupon" deals were the apex of industry innovation. Scanner technology may have improved inventory and supply chain management, and loyalty cards may have bumped up consumer loyalty for certain items, but neither offered sustainable competitive advantage. Recognizing the emerging trend to buy natural and organic products, Whole Foods' CEO John Mackey showed creativity and visionary leadership by tapping into consumers' desire for gourmet products, home cooking, and an emotional connection to their food and health. Between 2002 and 2006, Whole Foods opened fifty-one new stores and increased sales from approximately $2.7 billion to $5.6 billion. Now, even Wal-Mart has begun to sell organic.

IBM was known as the company that made "business machines" (as indicated by the last two letters in its name). So, Lou Gerstner was acting boldly when, in the 1990s, he shifted IBM's business model from computing to a global business services operation. The long-term strategy based on this un-IBM idea has successfully differentiated IBM from low-cost technology suppliers like Dell as well as traditional computing consulting firms like Hewlett-Packard. Under Gerstner's successor Sam Palmisano, IBM continues to push aggressively into high-end business consulting services and outsourcing aimed at CEOs and chief marketing officers (CMOs). By the end of 2004, the lasting impact of these bold ideas and actions was apparent: IBM's Global Services division accounted for 48 percent of revenue, as opposed to 32 percent for hardware and 16 percent for software.

Big Think requires vision and leadership. It requires questioning deeply held assumptions about a business or an industry, considering the business or industry from a new angle, and then acting on the new insight. Consider the challenges faced by organizations in the world of beauty products, opera, and online networking—and how Big Think leaders have addressed them.

Inspiration (Not Aspiration)

When Silvia Lagnado became global brand director for Dove, Unilever's skin care and beauty brand, in 2001, she was looking for a new approach. "There's no way you can sell beauty without aspirations, they told me," Lagnado said to me. But she

Newspaper article on Campaign for Real Beauty

Source: Daily Record (Glasgow). Used with permission.

believed that she could: by inspiring women to believe in their own beauty. To realize her idea, Lagnado had to challenge some strongly held assumptions within the company—assumptions that the entire beauty industry took for granted.

"We were obsessed with creating something big." The result: Dove's Campaign for Real Beauty. This bold idea debunked traditional stereotypes by celebrating real women of all ages, sizes, shapes, and colors as the new standards of beauty.

The campaign launched in January 2004 and went far beyond traditional advertising. Around the world, millions logged on to Real Beauty Web sites that expressed how people in different cultures view beauty. In addition to print and TV ads, Dove released a widely viewed, inexpensive YouTube ad spot that showed how beauty advertising distorts our concepts of beauty; "Dove Evolution" was downloaded nearly 3 million times in ten days, and thousands included it in their blogs. Dove did not stop at communications. It established the Dove Self-Esteem Fund to raise awareness of the connections between beauty advertising and young girls' self-esteem.

Keeping Opera Alive

The challenge faced by Peter Gelb, new general manager of the Metropolitan Opera in New York City as of 2006, is to keep opera theatrically and musically alive in this century. To do that, Gelb has launched a revolution at the Met. "We want to make opera true to what it was at the beginning, which is a marriage of music and theater. Our goal is to popularize opera without diminishing its artistic integrity," said Gelb.

Under Gelb's leadership, the Met is changing fast. Gone are the days of the stodgy opera house and its sing-and-stand style. A new wind is blowing from every direction. In his first year, Gelb launched numerous initiatives to capture a broader audience. The Met struck a deal with Sirius Satellite Radio to broadcast several performances live every week, supplemented by archival performances from the Met's rich broadcast history. Opening night in 2006 (a visually striking new *Madama Butterfly*) was broadcast live on a giant screen in Times Square in New York. The cast of a new *Barbiere di Siviglia* production performed the act-I finale on the David Letterman show. The Met's Web site was revamped to express its fresh, contemporary image. The Met has even gone to the movies, with Saturday matinee performances broadcast live in high definition at select movie theatres across the United States and abroad. Most important, directors of new productions are now chosen according to their experience outside of opera (e.g., in film, theater, dance, and other art forms), and silos are being torn down: artistic decisions are made jointly among the director, conductor, production, and administrative team. "All of this is creating a sense of excitement inside and outside the theater," according to Gelb.

Gelb is thinking big about how to establish new connections that shake the dust off the Met and transform the image of opera. In his first season as general manager, Gelb led the Met Opera to the first box office improvement in six seasons.

Two Lives Are Better Than One

Online social networking has been a huge growth business. LinkedIn is popular among businesspeople, but MySpace has been the biggest success story, selling for $580 million to News Corporation in 2005. Yet Philip Rosedale, former chief technology officer of RealNetworks, was convinced that there was still money on the table in social networking. Instead of connecting through personal profiles pages and friend lists, why not let people meet online, in virtual reality? He founded Linden Lab to create a video game–like environment called Second Life and left it up to the users to create their worlds. A 3-D modeling tool allows residents to build buildings, furniture, vehicles, and machines. There are no aliens, spaceships, dragons, or superheroes; Rosedale guessed that what people wanted was not total fantasy but another life imaginatively better than their own. Each user gets to create an alter ego, their "avatar," and customize themselves as they see fit, then step forward to explore and meet people in the virtual world.

After a quiet rollout in beta version, Second Life took off with a bang, growing exponentially since it grasped media attention in late 2006. Companies entered Second Life to buy ad space. Educators from Harvard University to Ball State set

Second Life avatar

Source: fotosearch.com.

up classrooms for their students. Reuters launched a Second Life news bureau. And Dell even sold your avatar a computer. Residents paid real money to buy "Linden dollars" that could purchase virtual consumer goods from Dell and other companies in this online world.

The future of Second Life is unclear, but the big idea of a virtual world is here to stay. Offline, I play host to the New York Video 2.0 Group (Silicon Alley's entrepreneurs of online video) to keep an eye out for the next Big Think online.

How Do We Create a Big Think Strategy?

Strategy is traditionally viewed as an analytical process, focused heavily on data and rational decision making. Books and articles on strategic planning offer a familiar list of factors to analyze.[1] For corporate strategy, those include:

- The business environment (political, economic, socio-cultural)

- The five forces that impact strategy in a competitive context: customer behavior, bargaining power, competitive forces, threats of new entrants or products, and intensity of competitive rivalry (see the classic strategy model by Michael Porter)

- Technology forces

- The resources and competence of the firm

- The resources and competence of suppliers, customers, partners, allies, outsourcers, and other third parties that the firm can leverage

These are not bad considerations. But using this kind of approach alone would not have produced IBM's, Dove's, or the Met's innovative strategies. For IBM, a situation analysis of this sort performed in the late 1980s would have surely indicated that competition was intensifying and that IBM could not grow, or even survive, by relying on computers alone. But then what? What could IBM do next? Similarly, for Dove circa 2000, the data and analyses would have indicated that Dove is a well-established brand with limited growth. Then what? Launch another brand of soap or shampoo? Analyses for the Met, as well as other classical music businesses in the early years of the new century, showed declining visitors and a lack of connection to younger audiences. Then what? Lower your prices for younger audiences? I have been in meetings with technology firms, beauty and cosmetics firms, and classical music organizations that struggled with these challenges. Using traditional market research and strategic analyses for what they are worth and not getting sidetracked by them is only part of the challenge. Yes, research and analysis may yield a valid diagnosis of the situation. But the real strategic issue is how to develop new and bold ideas to address the situation and how, then, to implement these bold ideas.

Think back in time to the Trojan War and Odysseus's big idea. The Trojan horse was a brilliant strategy and brought Greek victory overnight after ten years of Small Think stalemate. This was Big Think: the Greeks knew that the Trojans loved their horses. Why not give them the gift of a horse—a huge wooden steed that could conceal a few soldiers who, once inside the city, could fling wide the gates? Would traditional military analysis have ever factored in the passions of an entire rival organization to conceive such a brilliant and radical maneuver? Probably not. No doubt, the Greek general Agamemnon (like a well-trained executive) spent many a night looking at the numbers and doing analyses: troop levels, battalion formations, food supply lines, the height of the walls of Troy, wind and weather factors. But Agamemnon's battlefield analysis only led to tactical shifts in the standard siege strategy that the Greeks had employed for a decade to no avail. It took big thinker Odysseus to break the stalemate in that epic battle.

Let me be clear: asking questions and collecting data about markets, competition, customers, technology, and the like should be part of the strategy process. But data, spreadsheets, and analytical charts are mostly reactive tools that illuminate the past. They cannot envision strategies directed inherently toward the future. They are good for diagnosing problems, not for creating big ideas and powerful solutions.

Strategists at all levels seem to follow the mantra: as long as we do the right analysis, as long as we spend months in meetings doing SWOTs, number crunching, and traditional strategy maps, as long as dozens of consultants parade through the organization producing thousands of PowerPoint slides, as long as we do all that, a big idea and a long-term sustainable strategy will—somehow, magically, at the end of the tunnel— emerge.

Most of the time this is just wishful thinking, because there is more to strategy than just analysis. Bold ideas that change markets do not emerge from rote analyses that we perform like robots and that any competitor could do just as well.

In fact, standard strategic planning, which occurs at every level in the organization, follows a predictable process and virtually shuts out big thinking. Standard strategic planning, with its procedures, planning sheets, and analytical decision tools, with its endless meetings, buy-in procedures, and politics, sucks the juice out of any exciting idea, if it allows it to come to the surface at all. Knowing that anything too "out of the box" will not be approved by boxed-in thinkers, most executives censor their own ideas and do not even throw their big ones into the strategy planning pot. After all, in most strategic planning efforts, mediocrity is rewarded because it seems solid, builds on the status quo, and stretches one's imagination just a little bit. In these cases, Small Think prevails.

Once again, that does not mean that traditional strategic planning is all useless. Detailed analytical thinking can be valuable and is necessary at times. It is needed to aim for and achieve a clearly defined goal. It is needed to perfect clearly delineated tasks. However, without Big Think, strategic planning is limited. It lacks broader meaning and purpose. Worse, it becomes an impediment to visionary thinking; it preserves the status quo.

Formulating and Implementing Big Think Strategy

To generate bold and breakthrough strategies, strategic planning needs an alternative approach. It needs an approach that harnesses creativity to challenge conventional wisdom. It must transform the models that decision makers already have in their heads.

Such an approach starts with idea sourcing. Rather than benchmark competitors within our industry, we must go against the mainstream and look for new ideas outside our own industry. We must question some long-held but outdated assumptions, the sacred cows of a business. Rather than doing idea sourcing only internally, we must connect with customers in original ways and engage them to provide deep insights for our business.

The new ideas that we collect must then be evaluated and turned into a strategy. Throughout this process, we must avoid watering down big ideas. Operational factors and feasibility of the approach must be key considerations, to be sure, but we must remain focused on the big picture. The end goal must be a simple and powerful idea that creates new customer value. For example, for the iPhone, it was "creating a user-friendly and cool mobile entertainment product." For Whole Foods, "natural food with an emotional connection." For MySpace, "building a powerful community." Moreover, the idea must leverage organizational capabilities and connect the organization to other businesses and the entire market ecosystem.

Yet, Big Think strategy is not only about strategy formulation; it is also about strategy implementation. Big Think ideas must be clearly conveyed to employees and executed. The entire organization must be focused on Big Think. This requires leadership and processes that sustain the Big Think beyond a one-shot project. And that is the toughest task of all: centering an organization on the core idea—at the corporate, functional, and operational level.

Shaking Up GE and Samsung

When Jeffrey Immelt replaced Jack Welch as chairman and chief executive of General Electric in September 2001, he had big shoes to fill. Under Welch, GE was renowned for its focus on the bottom line—and getting rid of managers who did not meet financial goals. While Immelt inherited one of the world's most successful companies, he also inherited an organization steeped in Six Sigma that did not encourage taking risks and thinking big.

Immelt believed that GE would continue to grow only by developing new products and innovations, not by cost cutting and streamlining operations. This new approach included taking risks that could revolutionize the company. To do this, he had to tackle the very culture of the company. So what exactly has Immelt done to change the process- and measurement-oriented company into a creative powerhouse?

He started with a fundamental structural change in how managers and employees worked. Where in the past GE had a history of promoting from within, Immelt brought in outsiders with different ideas and perspectives—not only from other industries but also from diverse ethnic and cultural backgrounds to reflect the international scope of the organization.

For existing employees, Immelt encouraged managers to be passionate experts in their industries rather than expert managers who frequently moved between business units. He also fostered a culture of customer orientation. To Immelt, great managers were customer-focused marketers, not just great operators. The expectations of managers also changed. Under Immelt, every leader must come up with at least three "Imagination Breakthroughs" each year that are judged by a council made up of senior sales and marketing executives. And this is not Small Think stuff. Each breakthrough is expected to get

GE into a new line of business, geographic area, or customer segment, and must have the potential for at least $100 million in growth. Ideas judged to be worthy receive billions of dollars in future funding.

Many executives were leery of such fundamental change, but they are coming around. Business leaders have developed "idea jams" for generating ideas with people from diverse business groups. GE also instituted a "virtual idea box," where employees at all levels can propose new ideas via the company intranet.

A similar organizational transformation is taking place at Samsung. Not long ago, Samsung was known worldwide for manufacturing memory chips, cheap household appliances, and low-quality consumer electronics. In the mid-1990s, Samsung chairman Kun-Hee Lee set out to reposition the company as a cutting-edge designer of high-quality products, particularly electronics. To show that he was serious and that Samsung would stop releasing substandard products, in 2000 Lee arranged a public burning of $50 million worth of defective cell phones at a plant in Gumi, a town in central South Korea.

Within ten years, Samsung has become a global force in consumer electronics, surpassing competitors in the minds of many customers. Samsung employees now communicate and interact with each other very differently. Isolated departments and strict hierarchies have evolved into cross-functional teams with new processes that empower employees and allow them to bring new products to the market faster.

"At Samsung, we are committed to thinking big about the entire industry and the innovation that will lead it," D. J. Oh, CEO of Samsung Electronics North America, told me. "Over the last ten years, we have made amazing progress, especially in the U.S. market—and we are not done yet. Our new focus is not just about using great engineering to build new products; it is about tapping into the customer's experience with a great brand, through creativity. We call it the Creative Management and it is our new big thinking for the next decade."

The Six Strategy Tasks of Big Think

In sum, the goal of Big Think strategy is to leverage bold ideas and leave small thinking behind. Moreover, we must create the organizational structures and processes to support individual projects and keep the organization focused on Big Think.

The Big Think strategy process consists of six interrelated tasks. The first three tasks concern strategy formulation:

- Sourcing new ideas

- Evaluating the ideas

- Turning the ideas into a Big Think strategy

The following three tasks concern strategy implementation:

- Executing Big Think

- Leading Big Think

- Sustaining Big Think in the organization

While these strategy and implementation tasks may seem familiar, Big Think offers a unique approach, incorporating new methodologies and tools, for each of the six tasks. To remain focused on Big Think, we must employ this approach and not fall back into a Small Think mentality.

Sourcing New Ideas

Small Think strategic planning tries to source new ideas solely by analyzing a host of market and competitive factors. But for Big Think, sourcing really new ideas requires that we go far beyond this simple analytical toolbox. The creative tools used as part of Big Think idea sourcing are all about seeking new connections. We must find new associations by connecting seemingly unrelated concepts. We must benchmark outside our industry (not only within), question long-held assumptions (the sacred cows) of a business, and step out of the time frame of the present. We must strip down our business strategy to its very core to get more radical ideas. Most important, we cannot source ideas only from within the organization; we must include customers in the idea-sourcing process.

Evaluating the Ideas

Effective idea sourcing should generate multiple ideas, which then must be evaluated before we choose which to pursue. Small Think asks a small number of decision makers within the organization to evaluate new ideas according to their familiarity and similarity to past initiatives but never asks whether the idea will radically impact the business. To remain focused on Big Think, we should cluster and evaluate new ideas first in terms of their potential for lasting impact and whether they will change markets. Only then should we ask whether new ideas are doable. Ideally, the evaluation process should be as broad as possible, not only including expert decision makers.

Turning the Ideas into a Big Think Strategy

Too often, a strategic brief gets bogged down in corporate mission-speak, irrelevant data, and linear strategy maps, until the core idea is diluted by Small Think. Instead, Big Think demands that you capture your bold ideas in a crisp image that you further develop using the *four Big Think strategy quadrants*: organizational capabilities required, opportunities and challenges in the business networks, the customer value created by the strategy, and the role of the market ecosystem in bringing it to life. The strategy development process of Big Think resembles the score of a Mahler symphony: you are weaving your bold ideas into a dynamic whole that provides a clear plan for achieving your goals.

Executing Big Think

With Small Think, even the best new strategy can get bogged down in the execution: inertia slows the launch, the rollout is divided between silos (manufacturing, marketing, service) that never communicate, and the customer is nowhere to be found. Executing a Big Think strategy demands tremendous effort; it can feel as if you have to pull a ship over a mountain. Rather than getting buy-in from your employees, you must tap into their dreams. Rather than wasting time on aligning the entire organization perfectly around the strategy, you must organize flexibly. Finally, you must attract your customers' attention through bold communications.

Leading Big Think

Big Think requires leadership. It cannot succeed with Small Think's aversion to risk and focus on short-term results.

Leaders at various levels of the organization must have the guts to take on the Big Think project, the passion to stand behind it, and the perseverance to see it through to ultimate success. Otherwise, you may just as well let robots do the work. Big Think leaders have a broad view of how to instill fundamental change. They do not just have a plan; they have an agenda. To stay motivated on the way, they consult a diverse group of experts and move in different circles in their professional and social lives.

Sustaining Big Think in the Organization

The ultimate challenge of Big Think is not just to set up one successful Big Think project but to implant Big Think into the organizational tissue. For that to happen, we must break down Small Think's organizational silos to assume an interdisciplinary mind-set. Moreover, employees must view work as play, and play as work, and be entrepreneurial. We need employees who are what I call "Big Thinky Heads." These are people who radiate a childlike excitement about new ideas. To keep them excited, we constantly expose them to new information that is relevant to their projects and stimulates their thoughts.

Build the Trojan Horse!

SWISS 168, SOMEWHERE OVER UZBEKISTAN

I am still haunted by my conversation with the consultants. On the plane, I am trying to relax and get some sleep, but I still hear them. "Don't you have some methodologies and tools?" "We have a tough time thinking big." "Give us some tools that we can use." As I doze off, I see images—images of Greek soldiers. Soldiers pulling an enormous ship over a mountain. I hear march music, ländlers, waltzes, yet those sounds are distorted, full of angst. Suddenly, there it is—the gigantic wooden horse carrying the Greek soldiers in its belly. As though from a distance, barely audible at first, then increasing in volume, then pounding my ears, I hear a chant: "Build the Trojan horse! Build the Trojan horse!"

I wake up, soaked in sweat, feeling the calling in my bones. "Build the Trojan horse! Build the Trojan horse! *Ich muss es bauen!*"

This book is my answer to this calling. I invite you to join me.

– 2 –

Sourcing
Ideas

Steaks and Sacred Cows

I am having steak with my steak buddies at Peter Luger's when it suddenly occurs to me: "A great strategy is like a great steak!" I exclaim.

Think about it. The quality of a steak hinges on one single ingredient: a great cut of meat. Similarly, a great strategy depends on one critical ingredient: a powerful idea. Steak preparation is simple but focused. You dip it in butter or oil, coat it with salt and cracked pepper, and sear it over the hottest possible fire. Similarly, strategy development should be focused and spare. The big idea must

A perfect cut

Source: fotosearch.com.

face the intense heat of scrutiny. But a strategy should not be cooked to death.

My steak buddies—three other Columbia Business School professors and a medical doctor—are used to this sort of exclamation. Incidentally, each one likes his steak a bit different, reflecting, in part, his own personality and interests. Levav, the consumer researcher of Argentine origin, has a natural tilt toward the Argentinean style of preparation. Oded K., the supply chain guy, is very interested in the sourcing of the steak—where it comes from, how it's been stored, whether it's been pretreated. Little Oded (yes, there are two guys named Oded in the group) is an expert in consumer choice modeling, and he likes his steak medium rare, "but on the rare side, please." (Trouble making a choice, Oded?) The doctor, a prostate expert, likes his steak from a bull. Steak—like strategy—is a serious matter.

"Frankly, many corporate powerhouses remind me of average steak houses," I continue. "They take a mediocre steak, overcook it, suck out all the flavor, and then serve it with unnecessary garnish. Their steak is like those overblown, verbose PowerPoint presentations that drown everybody in hundreds of boxes and arrows. Worst of all, they start with a flimsy idea that lacks juice. Nothing ruins a steak dinner like a cheap piece of meat."

How Can We Source a Big, Juicy Idea?

I have seen leaders in companies do all sorts of stuff to generate ideas. Many have no systematic approach to source bold ideas. Some tell their team to sit down and crunch the data. Others use brainstorming sessions, where anything goes and a moderator records the ideas on a blackboard or flip chart, the pages of which soon paper the entire room. Then everybody votes with a Post-it note. Still others go so far as to hire a pianist to play pretty tunes to stimulate creativity in their managers.

Used in this loose sort of manner, these methods rarely generate any viable new business ideas. There is nothing wrong per se with crunching data, group brainstorming, or inspirational piano music. They may even be fun and include a free meal. However, unless these techniques are fully grounded in actual business problems, they are worthless as strategic idea generation tools. Why? Because of the nature of the creative process and how the brain operates. Therefore, let me first present what psychologists and neurologists have found out about creativity, and then show you a variety of new creative tools that I have used in my own work with companies to develop innovative business ideas.

The Brain's Role in Creativity

Psychologists have divided the creative process into four phases: *preparation, incubation, illumination,* and *verification*.[1] The first and the last phases are analytical phases. In the first phase, you prepare the facts and immerse yourself in the problem. In the fourth phase, you evaluate and verify the creative outcome. The actual creative ideas, however, are generated in the two middle phases of incubation and illumination. It is revealing that these two phases are described with terms that seem to conceal more than they reveal.

The notion is as follows. After you have immersed yourself in the problem, for a while nothing seems to happen. However, you are already *incubating* the idea; the idea is already inside you but has not yet reached your consciousness. Then, suddenly, often in a seemingly unrelated context, you have an "aha!" experience—the *illumination*!—and there it is: the creative idea.

For a corporate decision maker committed to Big Think, it is those two phases that seem most mysterious. The preparation (fact collection) and the verification phases (testing and checking) you do all the time, or you delegate them to others. But what exactly happens in the middle phases? How do you achieve incubation and illumination?

Recent brain research tells us that the development of innovative solutions depends on the ability to coactivate anatomically distinct areas that store different forms of knowledge.[2] When these distinct areas are activated simultaneously, we access the connections needed for creative solutions. When I asked Dr. Kenneth Heilman, professor at the University of Florida's College of Medicine in Gainesville and an expert on creativity and the brain, about the details of this process, he told me that a particular neural system, the frontal lobe-locus coeruleus, seems to be involved in this connection process. "Highly creative individuals seem to be endowed with brains that are capable of storing extensive specialized knowledge in their temporoparietal cortex, be capable of frontal mediated divergent thinking, and have a special ability to modulate the frontal lobe-locus coeruleus (norepinephrine) system, such that during creative innovation cerebral levels of norepinephrine diminish, leading to the discovery of novel orderly relationships."

Aha! *Memo to HR: check all applicants for their frontal lobe-locus coeruleus!*

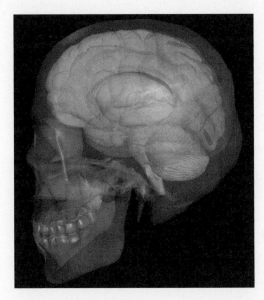

This is your brain on Big Think

Source: fotosearch.com.

But wait. It is not just that certain people are wired to be creative. Interestingly, for all of us, the neurological process of connecting different forms of knowledge seems to work especially well during certain activities—for example, sleep. That is why many scientists, writers, musicians, and athletes report that they had groundbreaking ideas in dreams and keep notepads and recording devices at their bedside.

- Chemist Friedrich August Kekulé had a dream about a snake seizing its own tail, which led to the circular structure of the benzene molecule.

- Stephen King claims that the ideas for several of his novels came to him in dreams.

- Paul McCartney reported that he first heard the tune for "Yesterday" in a dream.

- Golfer Jack Nicklaus said he found a new golf swing in a dream and tried it out the next day on the course, shooting a sixty-eight.

Should we be staging big sleep-ins instead of strategy meetings? Is there another way to activate different knowledge structures?

"I believe creativity can be 'encouraged,'" Heilman continued. "We have known for decades that when young rodents are put in a stimulating environment, they have a much richer neural network than their siblings who were not raised in this environment."

What managers therefore need are tools that encourage unusual connections in the brain. The following five idea-sourcing tools are all based on stimulating such connections (see figure 2-1). The first tool, called *combining the (seemingly) incompatible*, draws connections between the company and a seemingly incompatible concept—for example, an unrelated trend in the business environment. The second tool, *outside-industry benchmarking*, connects best practices from companies outside your own industry to your business. The third tool, *killing the sacred cows*, connects the underlying assumptions of your business to their challenges. The fourth

FIGURE 2-1

The five idea sourcing tools

1 **Combining the (seemingly) incompatible**
Company and unusual concept

2 **Outside-industry benchmarking**
Company and outside industry

3 **Killing the sacred cows**
Assumptions and their challengers

4 **Stepping out of your time frame**
Present strategy and future/past

5 **Strategy stripping**
Strategy and its extremes

tool, *stepping out of your time frame*, connects the present state of your business with alternative future or past scenarios. The final tool, *strategy stripping*, connects your current strategy with a more extreme version of itself. Using these tools just with your own managers is not enough. You must involve your customers. Therefore, at the end, I will discuss how to connect with customers in your idea sourcing.

Combining the (Seemingly) Incompatible

Consider the following brands and trends (circa 2007):

- Kellogg's Corn Flakes—and spirituality

- Chanel—and fear of environmental hazards

- Northwest Airlines—and health and wellness

One idea-sourcing tool I frequently use in my business creativity seminars asks people to combine one concept with another seemingly incompatible concept—for example, a well-known brand with a seemingly incompatible social phenomenon or lifestyle trend.

It is key to pair concepts that seem incompatible because they stretch people's imagination and facilitate the formation of unusual connections. Moreover, make sure that this sourcing tool is seen as a playful exercise; the objective is to generate ideas, not to evaluate them.

Here is how it works.

1. *Create a company visual board.* You divide participants into small groups of six to eight people each. Each group gets equipped with a stack of magazines, along with scissors, tape or glue, and a big sheet of poster board, and creates a visual board (a collage of images from the magazines) that reflects the essence of a brand—such as Kellogg's, Chanel, or Northwest Airlines.

2. *Create a trend board.* Each group creates another visual board—this time reflecting an emerging trend in society. These may include the ones mentioned above (spirituality, fear of environmental hazards, health and wellness) as well as, for example, small indulgences, online social networking, living simply, or Internet TV. For B2B companies, the trends could be business trends such as outsourcing, diversifying the workforce, or digitizing business processes.

3. *Connect the trend with the company.* You pair each company or product with a trend, taking care to avoid any obvious matches, and send everyone off into groups one last time. Each group is told to come up with a new concept marrying the brand and the trend,

including some kind of product launch, event, and kickoff campaign.

Here's where the boundaries really break down and the seemingly incompatible get combined. Rather than focusing on family and health, as Kellogg's Corn Flakes currently does, participants using the tool saw an opportunity to slow down breakfast time: take a deep breath and enjoy breakfast in a meditative mode. The team elevated cereal as a step along the path to enlightenment and recommended a line extension featuring spiritual imagery on its packaging. The group also proposed a Kellogg's-sponsored mass yoga event in a public park, where participants could gather for one huge yoga session followed by a healthful bowl of Kellogg's Corn Flakes.

The Chanel group capitalized on high fashion's license to go wherever it wants and came up with a new concept: "Fear never looked so good." The team envisioned a product line punctuated with work-style pants and heavy, sturdy shoes, and even germ masks—perhaps for air travel—emblazoned with the Chanel name.

The Northwest Airlines group debated how the airline might reinvigorate itself through a repositioning that taps into the health-and-wellness trend. The launch plan conceived an updated, more wholesome choice of snacks and meals, friendly group stretching exercises inside the passenger cabin during flights, and new destinations providing opportunities for outdoor activities. The launch could entail joint ventures with national health clubs to drive home the wellness link. A proposed slogan: "Land in better shape than when you took off."

I have used this tool in numerous sessions with executives from a variety of industries. What it invariably shows is that *concepts that may seem incompatible don't have to be.* The groups with the most successful results were willing to play around with contradictions, to consider the positive as well as negative images affiliated with a company, product, or trend. They worked hard to look at their assigned companies not just as in-house managers but also as outsiders looking in—to identify new ideas that might break away from tradition.

You can easily use this tool in your firm. For example, you can pair your own company with several seemingly incompatible trends instead of different companies with different trends.

Outside-Industry Benchmarking

Robert Forbes launched his company, Design Within Reach, with the goal of transforming the home furnishings market by making luxury goods easily accessible to a larger market. He didn't just look to the successful showrooms and interior design studios; those were the monopolizing, customer-abusing businesses he was trying to unseat.

"You must look around at other industries," Forbes told me. Breaking with the conventions of showrooms, middlemen, and months-long waits, Forbes instead looked at Williams-Sonoma's model for selling high-end kitchenware, and Smith & Hawken's sales of upscale gardening accessories and backyard grills. He also studied the success of luxury cars and how they created the right image and mystique around their companies.

The insights from outside his industry paid off. Design Within Reach caught on fast with its first catalog and integrated Web site in 1998; it opened its first showroom-style store (in company lingo, they're called studios) in San Francisco in late 2000, went public in 2004, and by 2006 had grown to a $160 million–plus company.

Benchmarking is usually done within the company's own industry or sector. That is, companies compare themselves against the best-in-class companies to identify best practices for new processes, methods, and tools, as well as fresh ideas. Benchmarking is supposed to protect companies against potential paradigm blindness. But does it really? Unfortunately, paradigms exist not just within a company but usually within an entire industry. There are better and worse car companies, no doubt. Sure, Volkswagen can learn from Toyota, and vice versa. Pfizer and Merck can learn something from each other. Likewise, the Gucci Group can learn from LVMH. But I doubt that this will ever lead to Big Think and industry-shifting ideas.

If you've spent much time with car guys, you know they basically all talk the same, think the same, have the same haircuts. Same for the pharma guys and the luxury goods execs. Within an industry, most people make the same basic assumptions about what customers want (the car guys say "the right engine and innovative features"; the pharma guys say "the most powerful drugs, of course"; the luxury experts say "*une expérience extraordinaire*"). They all make similar assumptions about how to compete (the car guys say "innovate new features"; the pharma guys say "speed up the pipeline"; and the luxury experts say "create *une expérience plus extraordinaire.*")

The same insular thinking is true for business gurus, too. We all wear the same haircuts (mostly bald or big hair or "out of style"), tell the same jokes, and use the same company examples. So when I'm trying to push my public speaking to the next level, I look outside my competition for inspiration. Jazz musicians, stand-up comedians, and talk show hosts are all great role models for me. From them I have learned how a speech is like a gig, how to use a sidekick for laughs, and how to run a lively panel discussion.

The same is true for companies. For generating Big Think strategies, whether they relate to manufacturing, new markets, human resources, or any another strategy objective, benchmarking within your own industry is not particularly valuable. You must look outside your business and industry. Only with outside-industry benchmarks can you truly overcome paradigm blindness and create market-altering ideas. When I work with American Express, we don't use benchmarks from the financial industry; instead, we imagine that American Express would form a venture with Amazon.com or W Hotels, and then source ideas that would have a positive impact for American Express.

Benchmarking outside your industry is harder than benchmarking within your own industry. Business practices can be quite different. Thus, the key issue is how to transform the best practice to suit your own industry. The benchmarking literature, unfortunately, offers little advice on how this can be done.

Here is a simplified process:

1. *Identify the Big Think problem area and come up with a conceptual model.* In this first step, you must identify the problem that requires new ideas (online customer service, the design of your retail stores, or processes for product innovation). This is important because benchmarking should not be unfocused background research or industrial tourism. You should

have specific guided questions; fact collecting and visits should be part of a structured program. Therefore, develop a conceptual model of your problem area; for example, what different types of service models exist online, and which ones should you benchmark?

2. *Set up a benchmarking team.* All the team members should be "open minds"—people who are truly interested in the problem area and open to new problem solutions. In contrast to within-industry benchmarking, however, they should not all be experts in the area to be benchmarked. Rather, half of the members should be experienced managers in the problem area, whereas the other half should come from related departments and divisions.

3. *Identify exemplary industries and companies.* First, find a list of industries in which at least two players are better than your own company in the chosen problem area. Do not be afraid of industries that seem very different from your own. They should be on your list for now. They could be removed later if implementing their idea in your industry would be unfeasible due to large structural or operational differences. Next, create a matrix using multiple criteria to explore similarities and differences to your own industry. On the basis of this matrix, prioritize which industries to benchmark. Pick the industry that is most similar to yours among those that excel in your problem area. The process for selecting exemplary

companies is quite similar to the industry selection. First, do background research on exemplary companies in the chosen industry that are particularly good in the Big Think problem area that you identified. Next, create a matrix that lists similarities and differences on multiple criteria to your own company. Finally, prioritize and select which companies to benchmark.

4. *Conduct the outside-industry benchmarking process.* The actual outside-industry benchmarking process is similar to other benchmarking processes. The phase includes desk research (Internet, industry databases, available case studies), company visits, process demonstrations, and management interviews. Each of these research tasks should be done by a subteam of at least two managers—one who is an experienced expert in the problem area to be benchmarked and one who is from a related department. Compared with conventional benchmarking, outside-industry benchmarking makes it easier to get new and relevant information and set up management interviews. As part of this process, ask management from the companies you benchmark to tell you how they would apply their successful ideas to your business. This can be done in individual sessions or, preferably, in group sessions. The more knowledgeable these managers are about your business, the better.

5. *Creatively map the insights and ideas to your own industry.* The final step is mapping key insights and ideas from the outside-industry company benchmarks onto your own business. This is a creative process.

You begin by sketching what these ideas mean for your industry and company. The goal is not to copy directly but to use the idea as a cue for generating equivalent ideas in your own business.

Recently, Vodafone, the global mobile phone company, asked for help in developing Big Think ideas to revamp the company's service operations for a Western European market. The company had already achieved the highest satisfaction ratings of any mobile phone provider in this market. But it had the vision to know that wasn't enough. How could it stay ahead of the competition and achieve the next level of success?

Outside-industry benchmarking was used as part of an initiative called Project Wow! by Vodafone. We performed outside-industry benchmarking for three problem areas: retail stores, call centers, and customer service in general. To structure the benchmarking, my partner on the project, Professor Sunil Gupta, and I developed two distinct service models. The first was a *service excellence* model characterized by personalization and intimacy. The second was a *creative experience* model characterized by excitement and lifestyle. Using these two models, together with us the Vodafone benchmark team identified exemplary industries and companies: the Ritz-Carlton hotel chain, Singapore Airlines, and Dell's B2B technology service site (the Premier Pages) for service excellence; W Hotels, Virgin Atlantic Airways, and the Geek Squad (a mobile technology service unit) for creative experience, among others.

The results were dozens of best practices and breakthrough ideas that Vodafone would never have gotten from other telecoms. From Ritz-Carlton, Vodafone learned how powerful focused service can be, even in a call center. Dell's

Premier Pages offered a model for new Internet services. From the Geek Squad, Vodafone could create ideas for a mobile repair service.

These best practices were mapped creatively to Vodafone's industry and its own customers' needs. Its new application yielded a set of bold new ideas unseen in its mobile phone market. It included a mobile squad for VIP business customers and a total revamp of the stores to make them more fun and high-tech, including live 3-D holograms amid store customers, new waiting-line management, and interactive screens outside the store.

Along the way, the company had to give up some cherished beliefs that had prevented it from thinking big. For example, it learned that customers do not want stores to be just selling spaces where the latest phones are displayed and customers are bombarded by service reps with tech babble. Indeed, in another Vodafone project in a different market, the store service maps were simplified around a new role—that of a friend—which entirely changed the way sales reps treated customers.

Many companies hold certain beliefs and assumptions that are rarely questioned or challenged. Those are the sacred cows of the business. To create Big Think ideas and strategies, you must challenge, even kill, those sacred cows.

Killing the Sacred Cows

CENTRAL, HONG KONG

Adrienne Ma, managing director of Hong Kong's Joyce Boutique Holdings, a prominent clothing designer retail chain, has been kind enough to get me a last-minute haircut appointment in one of the top salons in town. While I am sitting in the chair, the stylist stands behind me, swinging the comb and asking me the usual question:

"How do you part your hair?"

"On the left," I reply.

"How long have you parted your hair on the left?" he asks.

I had to think for a moment. "I guess since I was a little boy. Forty years?"

"Well, you won't for the next forty."

JEJU ISLAND, SOUTH KOREA

I am riding in a car with Hae-Sun Lee, managing director of AmorePacific Corporation. The company has two strictly separate businesses: skin care and cosmetics, and tea. As we are riding through the tea plantations, I ask, "Have you ever thought of putting tea into your cosmetics products?"

This question seemed bizarre to him. However, Lee is a creative executive and always open to trying new things. As he pulls out his notebook, I point out that nowadays customers are very interested in the antioxidant powers of green tea and other natural ingredients. "Interesting," he says and scribbles something down.

DÜSSELDORF, GERMANY

I am talking to the detergent and cleaning division of a major manufacturer on a hot summer afternoon. I start by describing my own day. I got up at 6 a.m., did some e-mails, took a taxi to the company (the air-conditioning did not work), waited in the reception room (no air-con there either), and now I am standing in front of the audience in a room (without air-con) on what proved to be the hottest day of the entire summer. Describing the remainder of my day, I tell them I will be giving another talk at a media company in the late afternoon and then must go to dinner before returning to my hotel.

"By noon, my clothes will probably be sweaty, and by the late afternoon, I will be quite uncomfortable. Sure, I could refresh myself, but I would still need to survive the day in these dirty clothes. So here is my question: do you have any product in your pipeline that will dry-clean my clothes on the go—a sort of mobile dry-clean detergent?"

Puzzled silence in the audience. I continue, inadvertently breaking several other sacrosanct rules.

"Why does a detergent have to smell clinical or chemical? How about a detergent with a natural lemongrass-ginger essence? After all, exotic fruits, herbs, and spices are all the rage in cosmetics and bath products these days. Or how about a detergent that through its scent clearly conveys throughout the house that laundry was done (an analogy to room fresheners or fragrances that indicate bathroom cleaning)? Could this be a sort of assurance that you have done your job properly, so to speak?"

Many organizations, like people, are used to certain ways of thinking, certain ways of decision making, certain assumptions that are so accepted that no one realizes that they are there. How often do you hear "This is how business is done here," "It's always been done that way," "It can't be done any other way." The engineers say that certain things are technologically impossible or financially irresponsible. The sales and marketing people say this is how consumers buy. The controllers and accountants assume that certain cost structures are essential to have a profitable business. The human resources staff says the unions will grumble.

When you challenge these assumptions, you will confront a blank face, or managers will throw up their arms, thinking you are out of your mind. Targeting patients instead of doctors—what? Opening a store for four weeks as a teaser and then closing it—what's the purpose? Manufacturing in the United States when you can get it much cheaper in Thailand—are you trying to lose money?

Killing the sacred cows is an excellent tool for generating wild and crazy ideas. Later on, we may have to adjust those crazy ideas a little bit because there may be a kernel of truth in what the engineers, sales and marketing people, and financial controllers tell us. Also, if you can't kill the sacred cows yourself because your boss will consider you insane, then bring in an outside lunatic to do it. Then test the crazy ideas with customers. If *they* like the ideas, you may have a winner.

If there hadn't been sacred-cow killers like Fred Smith of FedEx and Michael Dell, the majority of us might still wait all week for urgent business documents and buy a computer in a store. Fred Smith challenged the belief that long-distance mail cannot be delivered overnight. Michael Dell challenged the belief that people want to see and try out a computer in a store rather than online. Or consider Richard Branson, the British entrepreneur, who uses sacred-cow killing as part of his competitive business style.

If we step back for a moment, it is clear that the following are sacred cows in the detergent business that could be challenged one by one—and that cool new ideas could be generated to replace them.

DETERGENT...

- Comes in *powder* or *liquid* form

- Is used to *get dirt out* of *clothing*

- Is applied with *water* or in a *washing machine*

- Is used *at home* in a particular room

- Should smell *clinical, chemical,* or *fresh*

- Should indicate that it is *powerful and has done its job*

There are additional assumptions about how much a detergent should cost (nobody would pay for a luxury detergent, right?), how it should be communicated (through its functional features and benefits, not experiences) and distributed (independent distribution, yes; a flagship store, no). I feel that all these assumptions deserve to be challenged.

Challenging sacred cows can result in all sorts of new ideas. Not all these ideas will be great. Some will be silly; some too costly; some truly—at the current stage of technology and perhaps for years to come—unfeasible, or undesirable to customers. When I recently asked my MBA students to kill the sacred cows of a business school, they wanted to transplant a business school onto a cruise ship that roams the oceans, flying in faculty and business speakers by helicopter. (They still think it's a good idea. Perhaps I am too conservative here.) However, by testing and reaffirming assumptions, we can now gain more confidence in them. And a few breakthrough ideas may still lie beyond them. So, by developing alternatives to . . .

- The product form

- The product purpose

- The product application

- The consumption venue of the product

- The sensory impact of the product

- The perceived benefit

. . . we can generate fabulous, new business ideas.

I am pleased to see that major detergent manufacturers have finally begun to challenge some of their long-held assumptions and beliefs. In the United States, Tide has launched a collection of laundry detergents with naturally derived essential oils for a relaxing, refreshing, or romantic experience. In Europe, Henkel has launched an aromatherapy detergent. So, there is hope that some day, I may be able to use a real detergent on the go, rather than having to spray body deodorant all over my shirt in the middle of a hot summer business day.

As for AmorePacific Corporation, it has launched the Halla Green TeaXperience—a two-hour extravaganza of massage and intense antiaging skin treatments based on the antioxidants found in green tea—at its flagship store in New York City.

And since that haircut in Hong Kong, I have not parted my hair on the left ever again.

Stepping Out of Your Time Frame

Companies often are not only limited and boxed in creatively by sacred beliefs and assumptions. They may also be too tied to the status quo—that is, the present environment in which they are operating. Stepping out of the time frame of the present can be quite liberating.

In the late 1990s, Modo & Modo, a tiny company based in Milan, Italy, brought back the legendary Moleskine leather-bound notebook. The Moleskine has proved to be a huge cult hit, selling millions each year worldwide at bookstores, stationers, and other places where customers wanted to get in touch with their creative side. This fashionable lifestyle product is the antithesis of all of today's popular electronic accessories: MP3 players, PDAs, or digital cameras. It's a beautifully crafted leather-bound notebook for sketching and note taking. Importantly, it is totally analog, stubbornly unsuited to syncing up with the rest of your life.

Modo & Modo got the idea by looking back to the work and idea-sketching habits of creative individuals from the past. The Moleskine style of notebook, though not the brand name, had been used by generations of famous authors and artists (Hemingway, Van Gogh, Picasso). The result was an analog lifestyle product, a throwback to an earlier age. It tells you that you are a creative individual—in fact, part of a creative community—so you need a Moleskine to capture your free thoughts and sketches and drawings.

This retro product has also spawned special cobranded editions (such as the Van Gogh Museum Moleskine). A cult of loyal customers share their passion on blogs and in events like the Wandering Moleskine Project, a global participatory art project.

Looking back in time to come up with ideas is also common in fashion styles. Minimalism, for example, is fashionable every few decades and seems to alternate with its opposite extreme, ornamentalism. (My grandfather, a tailor, first pointed this out to me.) Later incarnations of minimalism are usually not identical to those of earlier times. Minimalism was a radical invention in the 1920s after centuries of ornamentalism, when Coco Chanel introduced the little black dress and the use of jersey knit for women's clothing, and popularized the bob haircut. In the 1960s and 1990s, when minimalism was reinvented, it had distinct '60s and '90s touches: simple, clean-cut London street fashion in the '60s and stark simplicity with a futuristic touch in the designs of Prada and Gucci in the '90s.

Looking to the past (that is, twenty, forty, sixty years back) and then thinking back to the present can be a powerful way to create bold ideas. You can focus on past consumer and business trends or on unsuccessful products and business models that were ahead of their time, or you can identify past customer preferences that may click again. This method brings creative idea sourcing to strategic planning methods that adopt a shifted time perspective (including scenario planning, contingency analysis, and futuristic projection techniques).

This time-shifting tool also works for the future. For an example, I am choosing a workshop I conducted for an energy company.

1. *Describe the current situation.* You first do a rough assessment of the essential features of your business in a broad-based socio-economic-political context, using SWOT analysis—that is, strengths, weaknesses, opportunities, and threats—but in a broad, macro sense.

2. *Envision alternate futures.* You sketch out three future scenarios: a future environment where fossil fuels are abundantly available, another one where they are quite limited, and a third with an extrapolated status quo. You choose a point in the future (say, ten years out) and start with the bright scenario. What SWOTs does it offer? Then you evaluate the SWOTs of the dark scenario, and then the SWOTs of the extrapolated status quo. Next, you generate ideas about how to respond to these future scenarios, taking into account the SWOTs.

3. *Think backward.* You list all the ideas you have generated in step 2. Many of them will be quite unusual and removed from the way you do business now. After all, they are responses to macro developments several years into the future. They must be changed to be actionable today. So now you must think backward. What would be milder versions of these ideas? What would be today's versions of them? What must we do now to make these ideas realities in the future? Make sure that the ideas, even when taken into the present, are still new, innovative, and bold.

BP's "Helios House" on Olympic Boulevard in Los Angeles is the first "green" gas station in the United States. The

BP's "Helios House"

Photographer: Tim Benson, 2007

gas station has been carefully constructed to reduce the impact on the environment, using low-flow toilets, solar panels, and a floor made of recycled glass. Customers receive cards that tell them how to save energy. "But you are still selling gasoline," I told Vinita Ramnani, Global Brand Manager of BP's Brand, Marketing and Innovation group. "Yes, we do," she replied. "However, with the Helios House in Los Angeles, we are educating our consumers and contribute to making the environment a little better right now. And there's more to come." Indeed, BP, formerly "British Petroleum," has rebranded itself as "Beyond Petroleum" and invested $8 billion in alternative energies.

Strategy Stripping

The final idea-sourcing tool, strategy stripping, connects your current strategy to a more extreme version of itself. With strategy stripping, you concentrate on the essentials of your business, the things you are already good at, and you take them to their absurd extreme, before scaling back just a little bit.

1. *Strip to the core.* You begin by listing all the elements of your current corporate mission and strategy (typically a list of one to two dozen, bloated with ambiguous phrases like "global vision," "quality," or "excellence"). Then each manager has to take turns making each element more concrete and striking from the list one strategy element that the company could survive without. When the list has gotten painfully short (usually one to three fairly specific ideas), then you have reached the core of your strategy. You have now taken off ("stripped down") nonessential aspects of the business, and the core is laid bare. For a retailer, that core might be "distinct personal service for high-end consumers," or it might be "iconoclastic product style," or it might be "sexy, cool brand image in the mass market," but it will not be all three. Hopefully, it will not be something as vague as "excellence."

2. *Go way overboard.* Next, you generate alternatives for radicalizing the company. For each core element, you ask yourself, "This strategy is all well and good, but what would it mean to take it too far? How could this strategy get us into trouble?" This is focused creativity that should yield radical, even absurd ideas. They may go "too far" because they would be illegal, impractical, or unprofitable. For example, if your core is distinct personal service, what attention could you provide your customers that would earn their admiration but bankrupt your accounts? If your company

prides itself on a yearly product line that is always different from everyone else's, then what about a strategy to create a product line that is so cutting edge that no one will buy it?

3. *Scale back a little.* Finally, you must scale these ideas back a little bit. First, look at what you came up with and see which ones spark some interest. You should seek some outside feedback here, from experts or from the market itself. Some ideas may be extreme but uninteresting. For each outrageous idea that attracts interest, you should now reassess what makes it off-limits. Then make a modified version that is toned down just enough that you might possibly pull it off. At the end of this step, you should have several bold ideas to consider for pushing your current strategy to its extreme.

Abercrombie & Fitch (A&F) illustrates how this approach can be used to generate bold ideas year after year. The company has pursued a focused strategy of being the top choice in trendy and sexy casual wear. There are many other brands that use a similar positioning, but no other brand has taken the concept to such an extreme. "Abercrombie," as the company is referred to casually, has been pushing the envelope of casual sexy apparel; the brand always lives on the edge, always considers how to take itself to yet another level of shock.

The controversies surrounding the brand are legendary. Whether it is a line of thongs sold for girls in preteen children sizes, nude models in its now-discontinued *A&F Quarterly*, or T-shirts carrying controversial messages referring to race, gender, homosexuality, or incest, Abercrombie's outrageousness has no limits. Hot guys became part of the Abercrombie style early on (after all, hot women are already overexposed in the fashion category), but they pushed this image to nearly pornographic extremes (think *Playgirl* beefcake in an L.L. Bean moose lodge). Abercrombie also pushed the clothing store concept to a new extreme based more on clubbing culture than on retail culture (such as Gap). The Abercrombie flagship store in New York City sports wood-shuttered windows that reveal neither products nor what is inside. At the door, a pair of half-naked male youths greet all comers with their winning smile and bare six-pack abs. Inside, the pickup club feel continues, with blasting music, three floors of dark rooms, pinpoint lighting, and hot-looking staff in tight shirts. To connect with trendsetting consumers globally, the company plans to open additional flagship stores in trendy cities like London, Los Angeles, and Tokyo.

Not all casual clothing brands take their business to an extreme in terms of lifestyle, like Abercrombie & Fitch. Other extremes may be based on cost-based sourcing (H&M), speed of supply chain (Zara), or specific service components (L.L. Bean).

What About Customer Innovation?

I described the previous five idea-sourcing tools—combining the (seemingly) incompatible, outside-industry benchmarking, killing the sacred cows, stepping out of your time frame, and strategy stripping—from a management perspective. None of the tools used customer input per se but used customer information indirectly. Yet, in fact, some of the best new innovations can come from customers themselves. You must involve customers.[3]

When Vodafone launched the aforementioned Project Wow!, managers knew they needed to learn more from their customers to "wow" them. They knew they had to tap customers for ideas on how to redesign every point of interaction to surprise and delight so that customers would stay loyal, tell all their friends or business partners, and spend more money on mobile services. Outside-industry benchmarking and killing sacred cows was not enough.

Vodafone's customers included personal consumers of varied ages and demographics and business users with diverse needs. The standard customer satisfaction surveys, however, would provide little benefit, because Vodafone was already ahead of the competition. So new techniques were created to get customers to think big and develop bold new ideas for the company.

I put Claudia Laviada, my most creative consultant, in charge of customer research. She and her team asked customers to keep a mobile diary of their life, using text and photos (taken with their phones) to keep records of every experience of using their phones—not just minutes and calling hours, but how and why did the phones fit (or not fit) into the rhythm of their daily routines? They took customers into stores, explored the environments together, and got them to role-play how they would like to be served there. They asked business customers to lead them through how they actually used the online interface, what their billing experience was, and what they needed to do before handing off their statement to their accounts payable department. They ordered new phones, called for repair services, and experienced services from the customers' side. Finally, they spoke with customers who happened to be service experts in other industries. In these ideation sessions, they imagined what great mobile phone service could be like. In total, Project Wow! sourced more than three hundred ideas from customers—some small and incremental, others break-through—that were clustered into seven major strategic projects transforming each point of contact with customers, from retail to purchase, to billing and repair.

Now, admittedly, this may sound like a familiar story. Nowadays everybody knows they should talk to customers to gain insight. For most companies, though, customer insight is just another ream of data in the quarterly pile collected by the market research team. The data may be qualitative, but they are collected in the same old ways: fielding surveys, watching customers, and conducting blue-sky brainstorming sessions. If this approach doesn't generate original thinking from executives who know your business inside and out, why would you expect it to work with customers who have used your product occasionally at most?

To source truly Big Think ideas from customers, companies must use approaches that stimulate the right kind of creative connections and idea generation, just as they do with executives.

How Do You Get Big Ideas Out of Customers?

Customer idea sourcing must be done in relevant settings; take customers to places and settings that you want to change. It must be focused on the actual decision situation; ask customers what they do, not how they feel. Finally, it must invite customers to be creative; ask them to imagine new scenarios, not evaluate the status quo.

Customers should be given an active and multisensory role, as was done in the Vodafone project. Don't just put them around a conference table and ask them to talk. Documentary devices like camera phones can liberate them to capture ideas in unexpected moments. Role-playing and theater can provoke dramatic new suggestions. The more freedom you give customers, the freer they will be to generate new ideas rather than rehash what they expect you want to hear.

It is equally important to involve executives in the customer idea sourcing. Often, the Big Think idea is sparked only when the customers' raw ideas and impressions collide with the thinking of executives. Egg and sperm—the two must meet for ideas to generate. That is, management, designers, or engineers must be personally present at idea-sourcing sessions with customers or even talk to customers directly.

Which Customers Should You Tap for Creative Idea Sourcing?

You want as participants customers who know your company and products inside out: the lead users.[4] Statistical sampling issues are not the focus here. Being statistically representative of the sample for the target market is beside the point. Instead, your customers should be fanatics who are passionate about the industry and product category.

Are you in the travel and hospitality industry? Recruit frequent business travelers. They use a lot of airlines, hotels, transportation services, customs and immigrations, and related services throughout the year. Don't just ask them about the small stuff of preflight, in-flight, and postflight phases. Engage them with the right topics: How could business travel be invigorating for you rather than a drag? What happens before and after your travel? How could companies turn the various service stations on your trip into mobile offices for you?

Are you a car manufacturer? Talk to your car nuts. In a workshop I organized for Volkswagen to generate bold ideas for the relaunch of the GTI, the company invited a sixty-year-old fan who knew the history and the car inside out—in fact, better than some managers. In another workshop for the relaunch of the Scirocco, Volkswagen invited a car collector in his late twenties who owned thirty Sciroccos and had to rent a warehouse to store them. (Otherwise, he was quite a normal guy.)

Are you running a small business, say, a steak house? Enlist your leading-edge carnivores. Steak aficionados, like me and my steak buddies, have new perspectives and fresh ideas about the contemporary steak house—ideas about the meat itself, the ambience, the music, the decor, the lighting, the steak knives—in short, the entire experience.

In sum, find those product addicts and brand fanatics who are already lurking in your customer base. Remember that customers can be end consumers or business customers, such as suppliers or channel members that you sell to. They will bring real depth and perspective that other customers may lack, plus a passion and freshness that may outstrip your own employees'.

How Do You Turn Customer Perspectives into Big Think Ideas?

Few of your customers will be experienced strategic thinkers, product engineers, or innovation experts. The raw material your customers generate must be examined for Big Think ideas by the team of Big Think decision makers. That's why it is so important that they be actually present, in part, at the customer idea sourcing. For the Big Think project team, what they see and hear can serve as stimuli, as creative sparks for their own idea generation. After the customer idea-sourcing sessions, use creative ideation sessions with the Big Think team to transform customer ideas into relevant Big Think ideas.

At these ideation sessions, insist that customer ideas get elaborated—not evaluated, criticized, and discarded. Assign roles to the team members. Give some of them the role of customer advocate to make sure the customer perspective remains strong. Give others the role of elaborators who are charged with building on the raw material of ideas. One team member can take the role of moderator, to keep objectives in mind and move the discussions forward.

Everyone Can Contribute Big Ideas

With the Internet and other new media, it is easy to invite anybody to provide new ideas. Idea generation does not have to be the assignment of a small team. Go beyond your employees and your customer database. Use the Internet to do a much broader idea search.

Some people you find that way may even be interested in helping you execute the ideas they generate. During the 2007 Super Bowl broadcast, Doritos aired a commercial produced by a customer. Dove followed suit during the broadcast of the Oscars.

Customers may be interested in coproducing the product. Threadless.com in the United States and bananapapaya.com in

China do exactly that. Customers design the T-shirts; the company manufactures them. Think back to the car fanatics I mentioned earlier. They would love to be involved in the production process of their own cars. Similarly, my steak buddies and I would take joy in coproducing a steak with a top chef.

Coproduction occurs on a regular basis in B2B markets (for example, in manufacturing) where it is referred to as "network innovation." Companies that leave the low-end production to other companies and act as assemblers and integrators need new ideas for this integration process rather than for the production process itself.

Ideas come from everywhere. The trick is finding the right ideas inside and outside the organization and creating a process that will constantly capture new ideas. The tools outlined here are extremely valuable for generating new ideas. Mine other industries for breakthrough ideas. Kill sacred cows. Look ahead and into the past. Strip your strategy. Above all, open up your mind and detect connections where none seem to exist. You may discover that Kellogg's Corn Flakes has more in common with spirituality than you ever imagined.

It turns out that John Harvey Kellogg, the medical doctor who invented corn flakes with his brother Will Keith Kellogg, was a Seventh-day Adventist who advocated holistic methods focusing on nutrition. He advised abstinence from sex, alcohol, and caffeine and adherence to a strict, bland vegetarian diet—with whole grain cereal at its core. This was the vision that drove the humble flake to become a core of the American breakfast, revolutionizing an industry.

-3-

Evaluating
Ideas

How to Dig for the Gems

WHEN I WORK with companies on idea sourcing, we often generate dozens of ideas in a short time. Clearly, some of them will not be as good as others, and even a large company could not implement every idea. So, how should you and your team go about digging through this pile of ideas to find the truly valuable Big Think gems—bold, creative ideas that are actionable?

To structure the evaluation and decision process, you first map out all the ideas by clustering similar ones around their common themes. Clustering the ideas is important because various clusters may require different evaluation criteria and skills as the evaluation process progresses.

Clustering the Ideas: Music at Starbucks

For example, let us say you are a senior executive at Starbucks. As part of a major new "entertainment initiative," you are charged with the task of developing an innovative strategy around music. Your team has sourced ideas from employees and customers worldwide, and the following ideas have come up:

- Starbucks could install jukeboxes where customers can select and play songs for a price.

- Starbucks could package a CD with a coffee purchase (a package of Brazilian coffee bundled with Brazilian jazz).

- Starbucks could offer a free music download with the purchase of a certain number of coffees in the store.

- Starbucks could have an MP3 station in its stores and charge a service fee for downloads.

- Starbucks could bring music artists into its stores for special events.

- Starbucks could throw coffee-music parties at its stores.

- Starbucks could have original music content produced and distributed through music stores.

- Starbucks could sponsor rock concerts and use them as part of a Starbucks coffee extravaganza.

- Starbucks could produce a unique music show for TV, podcast, or satellite radio distribution.

You could put all these Starbucks music ideas in one pile: "Starbucks and music." The company could have similar piles for the other entertainment initiatives, such as "Starbucks and books" and "Starbucks and video." Or you could cluster the first four ("music sales at Starbucks"), the next two ("bringing music to Starbucks"), and the next three ("Starbucks music outside Starbucks"). The latter approach is best, because each of these clusters may require different competencies from Starbucks and involve different competitors. The evaluation criteria that you will use for these clusters may differ. Later on, the three clusters may become part of a multifaceted "Starbucks music strategy." For now, let us keep them separate.

Now you are ready to evaluate the ideas one by one within each cluster. For the Starbucks initiative, evaluate each idea within each of the three clusters to determine whether the idea is worth keeping. At the end of the evaluation process, take a look at the remaining ideas and evaluate the cluster as a whole.

When you are looking for innovative ideas that will truly differentiate your company and have major market impact, you must set the yardstick high and keep it high. You may think you left small thinking behind. But often, even if you are sourcing ideas in innovative ways by benchmarking outside your industry, challenging the sacred cows of your business, or playing with more radical versions of your current strategy, Small Think will still start creeping in. Trust me—somehow, Small Think finds a way. It is always easier to choose what is uncreative, to propose something safer and smaller in scope, or to water down an innovative idea. Watch out for Small Think. Resist it throughout the evaluation process.

How do you keep the yardstick high? First, you must involve the right people. Beware of tightly organized committees and boards with bureaucratic rules and procedures. Second, trust your gut instinct. If your gut instinct tells you "there's something there," do not let analytical criteria kill the idea immediately. Maybe you are missing important criteria. Finally, when you use clearly defined analytical evaluation criteria— and at some point you should—start by asking whether an idea is big, and only then ask whether it is doable.

Beware of the Meistersinger Syndrome

Who should do the evaluating? "Expert decision makers, of course," you might say. Experts—such as the team or committee charged with the project—should be part of it, to be sure. However, they should not be the only ones, especially if they have been timid in the past and not managed a Big Think project.

For a great illustration of the perils of expert decision making when faced with innovation, consider Richard Wagner's *Die Meistersinger von Nürnberg*. This fabulous comic opera takes place in Nuremberg, the center of business and craftsmanship of the Northern Renaissance, in the middle of the sixteenth century. The story revolves around the Meistersingers, a guild of amateur poets and musicians who are master craftsmen in their main professions. The Meistersingers have developed a craftsmanlike approach to music making, with an intricate and convoluted system of rules for composing and performing songs: a singer while seated on a "singer stool" has to deliver a song where the verses are adapted to the musical strophes by a mechanical counting of syllables, regardless of rhythm or sense. They use these rules to make important decisions: whether a song is a master song and whether the singer qualifies as a Meistersinger. The group resists input from anybody else; after all, what do these nonexperts know about singing? When a new contestant, the knight Walther von Stolzing, delivers a novel free-form tune, breaking all the rules of the craft, they cannot tolerate his innovativeness. He gets rejected outright. Of course, after some maneuvering behind the scenes, and five hours into the opera, Walther wins the singing contest *and* the girl. Interestingly, as with so many creative ideas, Walther's prize song came to him in a dream.

The opera is also about Wagner, the innovator, and the difficulties he had as a composer. The "Meistersinger syndrome," however, is not just a historical phenomenon. Sadly, I have seen corporate boards and committees that act just like Meistersingers. They insist on absurd Small Think rules and criteria. They are insular, myopic groups that define rules and criteria based on how they have always done business. They are subject to groupthink because they do not seek outside input and do not vote on ideas independently. Bold ideas will not have a chance with them even if there is a clear business case for these ideas.

To avoid the Meistersinger syndrome, your people must provide evaluations independently and at times anonymously.[1] You may even separate the sourcing and the evaluation teams. Strive for impartial input and feedback. One of my colleagues at the Columbia Business School, Olivier Toubia, has developed a method to include employees more broadly: employees are rewarded for building on the ideas of others and can earn cash or prizes.[2]

Jim Lavoie, CEO of Rite-Solutions, a Connecticut-based B2B information technology firm with approximately 150 employees, has taken the approach one step further. Any employee can propose a new idea (a new technology, product, or cost-saving measure) by writing a proposal that outlines the idea and what the company can do with it. The ideas then become stocks in a mock stock market called "Mutual Fun," and employees can buy and sell the stocks. Stock price changes reflect the sentiments and intellectual investments of the employees. Every employee can see every day which ideas the company will apply in the future.

"The best insights often come from people other than senior managers. So we created a marketplace for employees to produce and evaluate ideas. Senior management takes notice when they see strong employee support for an idea," said Lavoie.

One proposal was to apply three-dimensional visualization technology to help sailors and security personnel practice emergency decision making. Top management was skeptical about the idea initially but turned around when employee support was strong. In 2006, that product line, called Rite-View, accounted for 30 percent of total sales growth.

Ordinary people can be quite good at generating bold ideas and even better at evaluating them. Involving ordinary people in the evaluation process is therefore important. If the ideas can be shared, talk to friends to test your ideas. Do not tell them your opinion. Do not reveal which ideas are yours. Get their unbiased view by asking, "Somebody suggested this to me—what do you think?" Keep the respondents independent and involve as many people as possible. You may even set up "wiki"-type pages to share evaluations and to improve ideas collaboratively as part of the process, thus achieving on a small scale what Wikipedia has done on a large scale.

Wikipedia: Tapping the World Brain

Wikipedia is a collaborative success story on a massive scale. Wikipedia is run by a nonprofit organization called Wikimedia Foundation created by Jimmy Wales, who described Wikipedia as "an effort to create and distribute a free encyclopedia of the highest possible quality to every person on the planet in their own language." In January 2007, Wikipedia boasted 7.4 million articles in 253 languages including more than 1.8 million in the English edition; it ranked as the eleventh-most-visited Web site worldwide and received between 10,000 and 30,000 page requests per second.

Wikipedia is independently written and edited by the public. Past edits of articles are retained and can be viewed any time. Continuous evaluation and revision is used to guarantee timeliness and accurateness. Many people initially were highly critical of this sourcing-and-evaluation model. Yet, academic research studies comparing Wikipedia with other sources (such as the *Encyclopedia Britannica*) suggest a high level of accuracy.

Where did I find this information? On Wikipedia, of course.

The idea of a collaborative knowledge resource, edited by the world, was not invented by Wikipedia. In the 1930s, the English science fiction writer H. G. Wells proposed the very same idea, which he called (lacking computers) a "world brain."[3] Now, every company can access parts of the world brain by setting up wiki-type models for idea evaluation.

Instinct + Analysis

Aside from avoiding the limits of expert judging panels, we can learn yet another lesson from the *Meistersinger* opera.

Good judgment is not only the result of including the right people. You also must use both instinct and analytical judgment. In their evaluations, the Meistersingers are obsessed with rules and analyzing whether a song and the singer's performance fit those rules. Only one of them, Hans Sachs, is a wise man: he sees the potential of the song that everyone else rejects. He trusts his instinct.

> *I feel it, and cannot understand it.*
> *But then how should I grasp what seemed to me*
>   *immeasurable?*
> *No rule seemed to fit it, and yet there was no fault in it.*
> *It sounded so old and yet was so new . . .*
> *If [the song] made the Masters uneasy,*
> *It certainly well pleased Hans Sachs.*

Can you relate to what he is saying (or, actually, singing)? Have you been in situations where something felt right, even great, but you could not understand or explain why? Big Think decisions are clearly emotional ones. They demand new ways of thinking. At the sight of such greatness, we are dumbstruck.

SINGAPORE

My fashionista friend Jin Han, a professor at Singapore Management University, sends me to Orchard Road for shopping. He tells me to have a look at the new Givenchy men's line. "What? Givenchy? That label has been dead since the sixties," I reply. "Schmitt, give the label a chance. They have this superb new designer Ozwald Boateng, a guy born in Ghana and raised in London."

I am trying on my first Boateng suit in the store. I am speechless. I sense utmost perfection.

If I had to analyze it, I might say: it feels perfectly tailored, a contemporized Savile Row cut. I feel my body, the shoulders, and the muscles in my arms, yet it is not an overdone teenage-tight look. The fabulous, slightly shiny fabric and dotted lining inside makes it a perfect day-into-night outfit. I could go on and on, but none of this occurred to me when I tried on the suit in the store. It just felt like a really creative, really different, cool suit.

TOKYO, JAPAN

After a steak for lunch and a full day of meetings, I decide to treat myself to a drink in the early evening. I enter the corporate building across from my hotel in Shiodome, take the elevator up to the forty-first floor, and go straight to the bar off the elevator. Nice bar: dark spotlights, a long bar counter in dark wood, and a fabulous view of Ginza, Tokyo's business and entertainment district.

I order a gin and tonic. "Yes, Hendricks, please."

The bartender puts down my drink, and I can't believe what I am tasting. "This is a perfect drink. And these are the most perfect ice cubes I've ever seen."

The bartender politely thanks me for the compliment. "Hendricks is a great gin, and I make the ice cubes every day myself." He pulls out one massive ice block from underneath the bar area. He explains in detail how he made the cubes, what water he used, and so on. Next, he pulls out a kitchen knife that looks more like a Japanese sword, demonstrating how he cuts the cubes. I can't believe what I am seeing.

Whenever I run into somebody who feels bored or blasé, I send them to that bar. "Just go there. Trust me. I cannot explain why. But it will change your life."

MUNICH, GERMANY

I am walking through the Dan Flavin retrospective at the Pinakothek der Moderne, Munich's modern and contemporary art museum. I am overwhelmed.

A lightbulb goes off in my mind. "This is a big idea. Outstanding."

When I tell other people about it, I have a tough time explaining why I think the show is so good. I talk about the way the artist uses fluorescent light installations to make his conceptual points about art. About the art object, for example. Is it the light source that is beautiful, or the light reflected? Is the art object permanent? No, it

Dan Flavin light installation . . . Aha!

Dan Flavin, untitled (to the "innovator" of Wheeling Peachblow), 1966–1968. Photo: Billy Jim, New York. © 2007 Stephen Flavin, Artists Rights Society (ARS), New York.

actually changes, depending on how the work is installed. And so on. It is not easy to explain. But when I see the work, I just know . . .

Evaluating big ideas is, in part, like judging a suit, a drink (and the ice cubes), or a work of art. A lot of evaluating is done on a gut level, and it should be. It is instinctive. People love certain ideas instantly or not. Of course, they can also step back and analyze, but they do so merely to justify their instinct. For many years, research on decision making was focused on preventing this sort of "irrational" behavior with rational decision models. Recent research, however, suggests that split-second decisions are not bad at all and not necessarily inaccurate. In fact, they seem to have their own rationality. So, by all means, use your instinct.[4]

However, no major corporate investment decision will be made on instinct alone. Gut instinct can also lead us astray. Therefore you must also use analytical criteria to back up our judgment.

When judging a new idea analytically, you and your team should develop evaluation and decision criteria along two broad dimensions: First, is the idea really big? Second, will it actually work? Importantly, make sure you evaluate the ideas in that order.

Big Think breaks with tradition, changes markets, shows real leadership. Only really big ideas should be retained in the evaluation process. Therefore, to keep the yardstick high, always start with the *big* question.

Which Ideas Are Really *Big*?

To make sure the ideas you have generated are *big*, use a critical eye, get outside opinions, and check each idea against three broad criteria of "bigness": creativity, business impact, and communications impact. You can also define more specific criteria within these broad categories or use additional criteria.

Creativity

Creative solutions are solutions that are new, innovative, or unprecedented against a comparison point. In evaluating whether an idea is creative, start by comparing it with what has been done in the past. Is your idea truly innovative and unprecedented? You can ask this question yourself, or better yet, test it in slightly disguised form with people you trust outside your organization.

To use a yardstick for innovativeness, compare your new idea with what your organization has done in the past. Is it really a new step for your company, something that has not been done before in some shape or form? Challenge yourself more: try comparing your ideas with what your direct competitors have created in the past, or with the ideas that players in related industries have come up with. Is your idea really that new?

Your self-test for creativity will depend somewhat on your industry and your particular company. If your organization is a laggard in innovation, you obviously must push yourself to do more than just "something we've never done before." But if you are already the leader in a highly innovative industry, you may need to look less at others for comparison. Again, outside assessment, in particular by management experts from a related industry known for creativity and innovation, is a good way to calibrate judgments.

In 1996, Carley Roney and her then-new husband, David Liu, wondered how they could build their own independent business. After a process of idea sourcing, they had lots of ideas centered around the concept of wedding. Their customer insight was that to many women (and men), wedding conjured up images of planning chaos, anxiety attacks over invitation etiquette and dress selection, and to-do lists that never seemed manageable. One idea cluster seemed particularly promising: creating a groundbreaking online meeting place for brides-to-be where they could plan their weddings and exchange stories and advice with like-minded women everywhere. They called it TheKnot.com.

Roney and Liu decided that their idea was, in fact, new and that the field was ripe for innovation. The multibillion-dollar wedding industry consisted of magazines that remained overtly focused where they had been for decades. The industry catered to twenty-three-year-old women, many of whom did not work, who were not paying for their own weddings, and who wanted to hear how things were supposed to be done within fairly rigid boundaries. People with different lifestyles were largely ignored. "Those magazines weren't modern at all," Roney said. "They weren't providing any new ideas."

The Knot Inc. took communications out of the tired old hands of the wedding industry and gave consumers and trendsetters a place to create and communicate new ideas about weddings. It gave advertisers fresh, direct, dynamic access to the wide range of soon-to-be-wed consumers.

The results? Nine years after launching, The Knot had become a publicly traded company exceeding $50 million in revenues. It is the most visited wedding Web site in the United States, with syndicated columns in more than seventy U.S. newspapers, a top-ranked gift registry, and numerous briskly selling book titles.

It seems to me that Starbucks' idea cluster of "music sales at Starbucks" also passes our creativity test. Would it be creative for Starbucks? Sure, and quite comparable in scope with other creative initiatives of the past (such as the "barista" concept, its constant introduction of new coffees, and the Internet access in its stores). Other major coffee chains do not do anything similar; neither do other casual dining chains, such as McDonald's or Dunkin' Donuts.

Business Impact

Big Think ideas have big impact. They change markets and transform industries and the companies that launch them. Are your new ideas really up for this task? To judge them, you must ask what the potential business impact could be if the idea succeeds.

Various measures and scales are used to evaluate business impact, depending on the tangible business objectives that are most valued by an organization (stock value, sales, revenues, market share, brand value, and customer lifetime value, for example). If you are comparing a variety of idea clusters and can generate meaningful business projections, you might put a numeric value on the measure you select (e.g., will the idea double the stock price, triple sales, double revenues, gain six share points, increase brand value or customer lifetime value by x?).

This will allow you to compare the expected impact of an idea against what your past strategies have achieved. In some cases, such as a start-up or realigning a company's business model, it may be hard to pin down projected numbers for something like sales. The business impact for the idea is judged by the potential to transform a company or even an industry.

Apple's iPhone was an idea that had great potential for major business impact. Many factors would determine its degree of success and how big the payoff would be. But clearly, when it was launched, this idea had the potential to transform Apple's already huge iPod business and to break down the barriers between the lucrative mobile phone business and the broader consumer electronics category. Wall Street acted accordingly: after the announcement on January 9, 2007, Apple stock soared, and Research In Motion (RIM, maker of the BlackBerry) and Palm (maker of the Treo) stocks fell.

How could Starbucks use expected business impact to judge the "music sales at Starbucks" cluster? Given Starbucks' track record, let us compare it against past successful sales initiatives. Projected sales could be compared against similarly priced merchandise items (like coffee mugs) and perhaps some seasonal (such as holiday or iced) drinks. A more complicated criterion would be to assess whether the cluster reinforces the concept of a "third space," the place where you have coffee, chat, meet friends—and pick up some music.

Communications Impact

Big Think stirs things up, turns heads, and gets you noticed. Will your new idea get customers talking? Will it make your competitors envy you? Will it get you on the cover of a major newspaper or magazine? (*BusinessWeek* and *Time* magazine do not print stories on incremental Small Think.) In addition to business impact, ideas should be evaluated for their potential for communications impact. Because they are exciting, even sensational, Big Think ideas often have the potential to generate strong communications. Communications impact can further contribute to business impact and provide a good yardstick for ideas that are hard to quantify in terms of business returns (for example, new business models, ideas capitalizing on broad economic or lifestyle trends, or innovative corporate repositionings). Here again, your evaluation should draw on external judges like customers, competitors, or the media.

Burger King's character "the King" was a move to differentiate the brand more clearly from McDonald's. The King capitalized on new media (for example, by setting up a "subservient chicken" Web site) and was a big idea that promised a big communications impact. Burger King knew it would be hard to quantify the strategy's impact on sales and profits, but its goal was to generate word of mouth. "Word of mouth is now a real-time constant in an ongoing collective conversation that goes on in the marketplace," Russ Klein, chief marketing officer of Burger King, told me. "At times, it is more important to be provocative than pleasant." The company felt that "the King" and "subservient chicken" could help it become part of that collective conversation.

For the "music sales at Starbucks" cluster, expected communications impact could be estimated by launching the idea in a test market and observing whether it is sticky. For example, will it be picked up online or by the press and create further momentum?

One last point: Big Think ideas often ruffle some feathers inside the company, especially among conservative departments like legal or accounting. So, if your idea causes friction within your team or more broadly within the organization during the evaluation process, do not worry. This may be a good sign that you are on to something big. Do not let naysayers kill your idea. Do address legitimate complaints and let legitimate criticism inform your thinking. You can't use your big idea to create a new strategy without first considering its feasibility.

Reinventing New Orleans

In October 2005, approximately a month and a half after New Orleans was devastated by flooding, CNN.com asked for suggestions from its viewers on whether—and how—the city should rebuild and how it could take best advantage of reconstruction.[5] Most of the ideas would clearly pass our "bigness" criteria: they are creative; they would have significant impact on the infrastructure of the city; and they would most likely have huge communications impact. But which ones would be feasible? For creating a Big Think strategy, ideas must indeed be creative, bold, and provocative. They must also be workable and actionable.

As you read through the following examples, ask yourself, Which ones would actually work?

- "Leave the areas that didn't flood as they are and make the rest like Venice, with canals for roads and the houses and properties on concrete islands."

- "Make some of the lower level districts into parks that would serve as flood basins if necessary."

- "Ask the Dutch government for help in building a flood zone. The Dutch build houses that rise with water levels."

- "Flatten the slums, build staff quarters, give the French Quarter and the surrounding areas to Disney or Harrah's and turn it into a play park for grown-ups."

- "New Orleans should be built in another location away from the sea level vicinity. I hope that the planning people use wisdom this time and rebuild in another section of Louisiana."

Which Big Ideas Actually Work?

For business ideas to work, they must be feasible, defendable against your competitors, and fit the internal culture.

Feasibility

Before knowing whether an idea is really ready to become part of a strategy, you must assess whether it has a chance of being implemented. What will the implementation cost? What other resources are required? Are there any legal or regulatory constraints? Big ideas should not just be dreams. They have to be realistic business ideas that create business impact and propel your organization forward. Do not assume that all will fall into place. Now is the time to listen to the financial planners, the technicians, the engineers, the detail-obsessed managers, and see how you can address their concerns. Be serious about envisioning implementation.

When Lenovo developed its strategy to acquire IBM's laptop business, it had to consider several factors to decide whether this bold move would be feasible. Beyond the costs of acquisition, the move would hinge on getting rights to IBM's ThinkPad product brand name and on reconciling the corporate culture of IBM's division with the Chinese company's own culture. Would that be organizationally feasible? "Lenovo went above and beyond what IBM employees expected," said Deepak Advani, senior vice president and CMO of Lenovo International.[6] By 2004, when news of the planned acquisition broke, the PC business was no longer a major focus at IBM. Thus, the former IBM employees, including Advani, were proud to be part of a business that would take PCs to the next level and invest in the growth of the business.

Defendability

To succeed, your idea must be defendable in the marketplace. Make a list of current competitors, customers and suppliers, emerging players, and threats coming from adjacent industries. Ask yourself how your big idea will stand up to these challenges.

Ask yourself how customers will feel about the idea. How will they react? Will they need lots of persuading? Will they be suspicious about the benefits to them? Try to see the idea from their perspective; if possible, do a quick customer survey.

Ask yourself how various competitors will react. Take their perspective as well. What if the competition came up with the big idea you are working on? How would you react?

Game theory provides an excellent, if highly analytical, framework for assessing competitive impact through perspective taking. Putting yourself in your competitors' shoes will help you assess the weaknesses of your idea and help you safeguard it against competitive attacks.

When David Neeleman launched JetBlue, his strategy was to provide a great travel experience at a low price. This was made possible with a new young fleet of planes, the latest entertainment hardware, and employees whose compensation was linked to the company's success, not to union contracts. This idea created enormous clout in the marketplace because the older U.S. airlines would not be able to match it, saddled as they were with fleets of older planes and large pension obligations to former employees. It also set the bar really high for JetBlue. When JetBlue experienced a major operational failure in February 2007 on Valentine's Day, stranding thousands of customers during a winter snowstorm and keeping them on the runways for several hours, Neeleman challenged the industry once again by issuing the first-ever Customer Bill of Rights for airline customers within a few days.

Internal Fit

If an idea is truly creative, has great potential for business and communications impact, can be feasibly executed, and can be defended in the market, you are probably looking at a winner. But you still have to consider how it will fit within your organization. Ideally, the idea should have a strong match with the mission, vision, and objectives of your firm. Why "ideally"? Matching firm mission, vision, and objectives might sound like a basic requirement. But if your mission, vision, and objectives are weak, diffuse, or uninspiring, then a really big idea will ultimately fail against those criteria. That, indeed, is a frequent problem.

If your organization is too convention-bound to embrace your great Big Think idea, then you may need to find another home where it can thrive. You can incubate a Big Think idea in an independent team within the company. The team may merit free rein to undertake it as a special project, an approach sometimes used for innovative product development. In some cases, you may even outsource your big idea to an outside firm with resources and expertise to execute it.

A Few Lessons from the Farms of Minnesota

Evaluating innovative ideas for Big Think potential requires balancing several factors: expert opinions versus outsiders, instinct versus analysis, and bigness versus workability. After evaluating our initial pile of ideas, we will hopefully end up with at least one cluster of ideas that we can turn into a Big Think strategy. If not, we must go back to idea sourcing and generate a few more ideas.

But what shall we do with the ideas that didn't make it?

RAYMOND, MINNESOTA

"Never throw an idea away; you can find a gem in all kinds of sh*t," advises Nick Peterson, who has been working with me for years at a research center that I run at Columbia Business School. Nick grew up on a farm in Minnesota. He took me to his hometown to demonstrate what he means.

"When I grew up on this farm, I shoveled manure out of the barn and into piles every day," Nick explains. "As a kid, I also used to go fishing with my dad and my Uncle Harley. There is nothing like a fat white grub worm for catching fish. The best way to find them was by digging through the piles of manure. Manure is actually pretty valuable, and not only for finding grubs. Come springtime, those piles of crap turn into fertilizer for that year's crop."

"So what you are saying, Nick, is that digging for grub worms is a lot like idea evaluation at companies," I comment. "There are often several valuable ideas to pick out from the pile—and what is left over can be saved as fertilizer for a later project."

"You can even sell the stuff to other farmers who do not raise livestock," Nick adds. "Nowadays, this can be very easy and convenient. Dairy farms have a conveyer system that runs under the back ends of the cows in the milking stalls. The cow does its business, and it is whisked away into a manure pond outside the barn or put on trucks and transported away."

Nick is right, of course. If you are clever, you can even sell your leftover ideas to other businesses (suppliers, retailers, or other channel members). In one Big Think consulting project that I led for a cosmetics firm, the team generated several innovative ideas that were outside the scope of its mandate—particularly ideas regarding the retail environment. So they handed the ideas off to the company's retail division, which turned them into a new strategy to improve the store environment and grow its business.

So, What Happened to Starbucks' Music Initiative?

Over the last few years, Starbucks has implemented several bold ideas to make a move into the music business. In 1999, it bought the retail music chain Hear Music and announced new Hear Music Starbucks locations where, for a fee, consumers could burn their own CDs from a library of over two hundred thousand songs. It has also coproduced exclusive albums available only at Starbucks, such as the 2004 hit *Genius Loves Company*, by the late Ray Charles, along with selling popular albums from stars like Norah Jones, the Rolling Stones, Bob Dylan, and Paul McCartney.

These initiatives have not been an unequivocal success. After two years of testing CD-burning kiosks in Washington and California, Starbucks pulled them from all but a handful of stores due to lack of use. At the time of this book's writing, the company insists it is not giving up on the music business. In fact, it has had several successes in selling CD compilations and selected titles from major artists. Starbucks may also be retooling to launch a new in-store digital music service compatible with portable music players. Executives seem to feel strongly that the idea of pairing music with Starbucks is the right one.

Instinctively, and using several analytical criteria, the connection between coffee and music indeed feels right. However, success is not necessarily guaranteed if we just experiment with one great idea after another. Instead, we must turn the music ideas into a coherent music strategy that delivers a value-adding experience for the consumer. How can Starbucks deploy its organizational capabilities to deliver such an experience? Does it have the people who can pull it off? Is the company prepared to make new resources available? Also, who are the right partners for the music venture? How could Starbucks build a community around music that will help its coffee sales?

Addressing these questions means moving from a set of great ideas to formulating a Big Think strategy.

Turning Ideas
into Strategy

What Would Mahler Do?

MANY COMPANIES SPEND a lot of energy developing and evaluating new and innovative ideas. But having a bunch of great ideas is not a focused strategy. There is still more work to be done to turn your ideas into a Big Think strategy.

Let us say you and your team have sorted and evaluated your ideas. You have selected your best—perhaps not just one idea but a few ideas, or a cluster of ideas. Some of your ideas may still be rough, a little vague, or unfinished, but you can already see where they are going. You can see the outlines of a Big Think strategy, although you must work out some details before you have a strategic plan that you can implement. As a start, try to boil down your ideas into a crisp and coherent concept in your mind and then capture the strategy concept in a simple phrase, a short description, or a couple of visual images (photographs or sketches).

Capturing Your Strategy Concept

TOKYO, JAPAN

The e-mail came to me from ADK, the third-largest Japanese ad agency, which I had been consulting with for several years. Its first paragraph put the issues succinctly: "There are so many discussions in the US and here in Japan that mass media will weaken drastically and that web 2.0/CGM/WOM/360/BTL [whatever!] will increase in importance. Our question is if there is any Big Think strategy or groundbreaking solution for this landslide shift in the advertising business. What is the next big breakthrough if any?" The e-mail concluded in a very Japanese way: "We would be more than happy to listen to your opinion about the above question, if you were comfortable to think of it."

Before I present my "opinion," I am reclining on a chaise longue in my room on the thirty-fourth floor of the Royal Park Hotel in the Shiodome district. Still pondering the issues, I gaze through the window that faces onto the headquarters of Dentsu, Japan's largest advertising agency—a giant monstrosity of a corporate building, complete with a theater and sky-top restaurants. All at once, this building comes to represent to me the old communication model that ad agencies in Japan, and elsewhere, are now struggling with: the model of a "communication blasting machine," which promotes one-way company communications to customers and generates revenues through mass media buying.

The next day, I have lunch with Koichiro Naganuma, CEO of ADK. Appropriately, "Naga," as he is referred to, has chosen a steak house to discuss the strategy for his company. The Japanese regard red meat that is extensively and finely marbled with pure white fat as the top grade of beef. This marbling is achieved by preventing the animals from grazing. Instead, they live in barns their entire lives. Moreover, they are massaged with oil and a special straw brush to improve the distribution and softness of the subcutaneous fat.[1]

Japanese cow being massaged

© Craig Walsh, Lucies Farm Ltd.

As we are having the steak, Naga talks about his strategy concept for ADK as a "new wave agency" that is more innovative and swifter than an agency the size of Dentsu. This is a concept that he has been using for several years, especially when talking to the investor community. That day, though, he presents his ideas more clearly than ever before. "The old communication model is broken," he declares. He continues, saying that agencies must change, that they need new sources of revenue, that they must give up their internal siloed structures of creative, media planning, and account management. Somebody should be directly in touch with the client, perhaps be at the client site all the time, like consultants. Naga is on a roll, bullish. Isn't it amazing what a great piece of Japanese meat can do?

Later on that day, I finally present my opinion. I project an image of the Dentsu corporate tower in the background of a slide reading, "The old model: Communication blasting machine." I then switch to another slide, describing an agency as an interactive "communication negotiator" between the company and the consumer. The agency will not push communications onto consumers; it will take on a strategic-advisory as well as executional role, counseling client companies on how to manage the relationship with consumers at various communication touch points.

COLUMBUS CIRCLE, NEW YORK CITY

A week later, I meet Naga again, this time for black coffee at the Mandarin Oriental Hotel on Columbus Circle. He brings up the images of communication blasting machine versus communication negotiator again. This contrast has struck a chord. To be sure, if it were adopted as a strategy for the agency, the agency would need to work out a number of strategy and implementation details, perhaps even change the term. However, some possible ideas for the future have been uncovered, and these ideas have been captured in a strategy concept, which could provide guidance for the strategy development process that might follow.

Developing Your Big Think Strategy: The Four Quadrants

Once you have a strategy concept and thus the broad outlines of a strategy, you can develop your strategy further by using what I call the "four Big Think strategy quadrants." The four quadrants are created by two dimensions—an *organizational*-versus-*market* dimension (that is, what must happen in your organization to deliver the strategy and what must happen in the marketplace) and a *singular*-versus-*systemic* dimension (referring to individual efforts versus collaborative efforts).[2] Developing your ideas into a strategy means answering the key question posed by each quadrant.

As shown in figure 4-1 the four strategy quadrants are:

- *Organizational/singular.* What *organizational capabilities* must we invent, reinvent, or redo to deliver the Big Think strategy, and how should we employ them to make the strategy a success?

- *Organizational/systemic.* What *business networks* (partners in the supply chain as well as alliances and

FIGURE 4-1

The four Big Think strategy quadrants

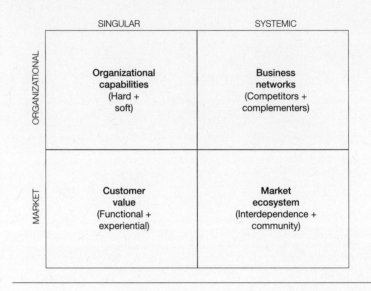

other forms of collaborations) can we use, and how should we use them, to make the strategy a success?

- *Market/singular.* What kind of *customer value* can the strategy create for various customer segments, and how can we deliver this customer value?

- *Market/systemic.* What kind of *market ecosystem* can we create, and how can we use it to enhance the strategy?

Organizational capabilities concern both hard competencies (such as manufacturing, technical, investment) as well as soft ones (such as human resources). For example, Dell Computer's Big Think strategy of competing with made-to-order personal computers (rather than stocking standard models in stores), which was very successful in the 1990s, required a specific set of organizational skills in its product development, marketing, and, most important, supply chain. Similarly, as Google grows and further expands beyond text search, it will need to ask itself what hard and soft competences it must deliver on its strategy.

Business networks include both competitors and complementary business partners. For example, fashion company Zara's strategy was built on offering extremely fast market releases of new products based on luxury brands of that season. This strategy takes advantage of certain key competitors (the luxury brands), but it also hinges on Zara's ability to work exceptionally quickly with the suppliers it partners with around the world.

Google, too, as part of its Big Think strategy to make all sorts of information searchable and available to anyone anywhere at any time, will need to scan the competitive landscape to determine how new upstarts (similar to YouTube, which Google acquired) may be an opportunity or a threat to its business model. Google will need to assess how it can work best with business partners, for example, in the media and communication businesses.

Customer value includes both functional and experiential values for customers. For example, the strategic plan of the MINI car was based on not just offering customers a compact car with exceptional gas mileage (a functional value) but also offering image-conscious customers an experience of retro, cool, and style.

Similarly, Google may not be able to rely on its search infrastructure alone to deliver value in the future. In what other ways could it create value, then? There may be experiential value in how information is presented (for example, by presenting text, images, blog, video, and Wikipedia outcomes at the same time). Also, there is value for advertisers if Google can drive demand by developing new ways of presenting information while still maintaining consumer trust and reliance. Like MINI, Google may also need to sustain its image of "cool" so that it can continue to attract a young and tech-savvy user base. Keeping this cachet will be increasingly difficult as Google becomes a corporate conglomerate.

Market ecosystem concerns interdependence and a sense of community among customers. For example, the strategies of both MySpace and the game Second Life rely on growth driven by a community of users who create their own content, network with friends, and thus expand the reach of the business. Google, too, must strategize about its market ecosystem, including both consumers and, for example, small businesses that use its services.

Here is an example of how the four quadrants can be used to develop a Big Think strategy for a multiple sclerosis (MS) medication. MS is a chronic inflammatory disease of the central nervous system. Its exact cause is not known, and it is not yet curable. Life expectancy used to be much lower for MS patients but is now roughly equal to that of unaffected people. Symptoms include changes in sensation, muscle spasms, complete or partial loss of vision, and bladder difficulty. Various disease-modifying treatments exist (such as treatment with interferons) and have been approved by the Food and Drug Administration in the United States. Because of multiple symptoms, treatments are usually supplemented with medication that prevents spasms, fatigue, depression, urinary tract infections, and erectile dysfunction. Unexpected attacks can be followed by periods of no symptoms at all.

MS patients, like other patients with serious diseases, are extremely knowledgeable about their disease and its treatments. They are often part of strong online communities and tell their life stories openly to one another. MS is not only a physical ailment, it is an enormous strain on the lives of patients and those close to them.

Let us imagine a Big Think strategy that is based on this key patient insight. The new strategy concept "From MS drug to lifestyle concept" is shown in the center of figure 4-2. The new strategy concept views the MS medical treatment, in part, as a lifestyle and social network support tool for MS patients.

FIGURE 4-2

Big Think strategy for multiple sclerosis

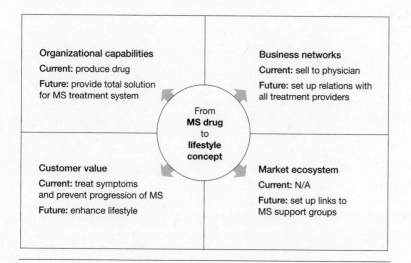

Figure 4-2 shows the key required organizational capabilities, business networks, customer value, and market ecosystem for the strategy to be a success. Some of the required resources may currently be in place or mostly in place; others may need to be developed in the future for the strategy to succeed.

Currently, the pharmaceutical companies offering MS medication—like the industry in general—are largely focused on product features and technologies (and not on lifestyle) and view physicians (rather than patients) as their key customer targets. The action plan and execution that could be developed through the new strategy, concentrating on patients and their lives, thus would offer a bold deviation from the typical product- and physician-focused approach common in strategies for MS medications.

As you develop your strategy using the four quadrants, you are no longer just looking at one or several ideas. You are weaving your brilliant ideas into a whole that will end up as a clear and compelling strategic plan to achieve your goals. Once you are done, you should ask yourself which generic Big Think strategy type you are following. If you use one type of strategy versus another, you will be facing and creating different market and competitive conditions. Being clear about your strategy type will help you plan how to act—and react—toward competitors.

The Four Big Think Strategy Types

In the traditional strategy literature, Michael Porter proposed three generic strategy types that can be found across industries again and again: cost leadership, differentiation, and focus.[3]

Other strategy thinkers have proposed their own generic strategies or "value disciplines"—for example, operational excellence, product innovation, and customer intimacy.[4]

A company can pursue these generic strategy types for ordinary strategies. However, it is difficult to develop Big Think strategies using them. Big Think is not about ordinary strategy. It is about rethinking your business. Often, you must combine or contrast traditional strategies, or take them to an extreme, or surpass them entirely. For Big Think, you need a broad-based model that lays out how new ideas relate to prior business practice. Do they challenge a business or industry's established conventions? Do they incorporate a new practice into an existing one? Do they take an existing practice to its ultimate extreme? Do they move far beyond the boundaries of an existing practice and transcend it?

Thus, I am proposing four new generic strategy types for Big Think: opposition, integration, essence, and transcendence. All these approaches are Big Think, but they are Big Think in different ways—and they are more or less risky.

THE OPPOSITION STRATEGY. This strategy type creates the opposite of established business strategies in an industry— sometimes in a diametrically opposed way, sometimes close to that. The strategy I outlined for the MS medication was an opposition strategy—juxtaposing patients with physicians, lifestyle with product features. The strategy of the MINI car brand was also an opposition strategy. The small car became a huge success worldwide at a time when the entire auto industry was obsessed with giant SUVs. Or consider the "do-it-yourself" concept. In many industries, business is about serving customers. The do-it-yourself concept is exactly the opposite of the normal way of doing business and providing service. This concept has been successfully applied for furnishings (IKEA) as well as in retail banks, airline check-ins, and hotel checkouts.

THE INTEGRATION STRATEGY. This strategy type brings seemingly incompatible concepts together, thus proving that they were not quite as incompatible, as polar or oxymoronic, as previously thought. It is possible to provide great service at low cost, to secure wide distribution of a luxury item, or to produce high quality at fast speed. You do not have to be stuck in the middle between a focus on cost and differentiation, or operational excellence and customer intimacy. The trick about this strategy type is not just that two seeming opposites are brought together; the Big Think is hidden in the *how*. Great service can be provided efficiently and at low cost by rethinking what service means (not necessarily a human touch—look at Amazon.com). Luxury items can be made widely available by changing them from having an elitist status to being broadly desirable, branded fashion symbols (see Prada and Gucci). High-quality products can be produced at fast speed by moving from handcrafting objects to producing them with precision instruments and machines.

THE ESSENCE STRATEGY. The term *essence* refers to the indispensable, essential parts of an entity, taken to an extreme. There are many examples of essence strategies. Wal-Mart, the largest discount retailer in the United States, is the essence of a low-priced retailer, squeezing out cost wherever possible.

Whole Foods is the essence of "natural." Google is the ultimate search engine without all the clutter of other search portals. To use an essence strategy, you need complete control over essential capabilities. For example, Abercrombie & Fitch, the essential sexy, casual clothing retailer, has full control over the design and production of its merchandise, stores, and marketing.

THE TRANSCENDENCE STRATEGY. The term *transcendence* is associated with "surpassing" and "being above the ordinary range of things." Transcendence has an "outer world" quality to it and is at a higher level. In a business strategy context, we can use the term to refer to a strategy that goes far beyond the established boundaries of the business and its industry. The BlackBerry transcended the industry boundaries of mobile voice communications and short text messaging by making e-mail available outside the office and the home. Nobel Prize winner Muhammad Yunus's idea of Grameen Bank, which offers microcredit to the poor—and makes a profit on it— transcended the credit business and the way we think about economic development. Richard Branson's Virgin Galactic business plan for recreational space flights goes far beyond ordinary air travel, creating a once-in-a-lifetime experience.

The four strategy types emerge, in part, from different idea-sourcing techniques. An opposition strategy frequently emerges from questioning long-held assumptions (the sacred cows) of your industry. An integration strategy often results from methodologies that combine seemingly incompatible ideas and business practices or from tools that bring in the past or the future. An essence strategy is the result of taking an existing approach to its extreme. A transcendence strategy frequently occurs when you benchmark other industries and then apply their business practices creatively to your own industry.

However, the correspondence between idea sourcing and strategy type is not one-to-one. Outside-industry benchmarking ideas can also lead to an opposition or integration strategy—not only to transcendence. Similarly, stepping out of the time frame of the present to generate new ideas can lead to retro opposition or result in a futuristic transcendence strategy.

Which strategy type is most desirable for your business? I suggest you take into account two key considerations: first, how easy it is to focus on one of the four strategy quadrants discussed earlier, and, second, how much risk you are willing to tolerate.

For any Big Think strategy, you need to fill in the four quadrants; however, depending on the strategy type, your strategy needs to pay particular attention to a certain quadrant. Specifically, when you use an essence strategy, you must, first and foremost, pay attention to perfecting organizational capabilities. An opposition strategy requires that you fully understand what new customer value you create. An integration strategy requires the use of business networks. Finally, a transcendence strategy requires that the market as a whole—that is, the market ecosystem—responds positively.

Also, all Big Think is risky. However, the four generic strategy types differ in their *relative* risk when we compare them with each other. The first two strategy types, opposition and integration, are likely to attract strong and immediate competitive reactions. In both cases, a company infringes on the turf of established players in the market. The latter two strategies are more subtle in their impact. An essence strategy does not infringe on others but only takes established market conditions to their extremes, and a transcendence strategy creates a new space that is currently not occupied by any player in a major way. As a result, competitive reactions will be weaker and less immediate. The strategy types also differ in terms of whether we must acquire new internal capabilities or whether existing ones are sufficient. Essence and integration strategies can usually rely on existing capabilities; opposition and transcendence need new ones.

Thus, the least risky strategy type is essence (relying on existing resources and provoking only weak competitive reactions). Opposition is the most risky strategy (requiring new capabilities and provoking strong competitive reactions). Integration and transcendence fall between the two extremes of riskiness. (See figure 4-3.)

FIGURE 4-3

Four types of Big Think strategy

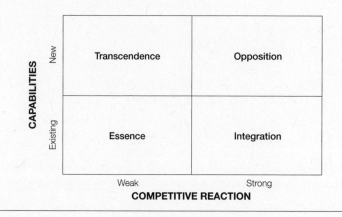

Note that over time a company's strategy may evolve from one type into another. For example, a strategy may start out as the opposite of an established idea, then become the essence of the new idea, then integrate with the old approach and ultimately transcend it. Sounds philosophical? Actually, the iPod, together with iTunes, has already gone through these strategy phases. In the beginning, Apple integrated two ideas that had been seen as polar opposites: digital music downloads and legally purchased music. Once Apple had established the business model, the iPod, smaller and more versatile with each generation, became the essence of the portable MP3 player. With podcasts and TV shows, Apple is beginning to integrate more traditional home media (like radio and TV) and, at the same time, transcend the entire category by expanding to live TV, mobile phones, and video communications.

So, when you step back and flesh out your strategy, ask yourself, Which strategy type, or combination, will your Big Think idea embody? This is important because it helps you assess the relative risk of your strategy and fine-tune the strategy accordingly.

You have now captured the strategy in a phrase or image. You have broadly developed the various elements of your strategy using the four quadrants and assessed its risk by examining it against the four generic strategy types. Are you done? Can you move on to execution? Not quite yet. You still have to develop the various strategy elements (as they are laid out, for example, in the four quadrants) further and, most important, you have to put them in sequence. What you will do is similar to what composers do when they develop a musical symphony. Like a composer who turns musical ideas into a musical score, you need to flesh out your strategy into a full-fledged strategy score.

Let's see what we can learn from a great composer about composing our own Big Think strategy score.

What We Can Learn from Mahler for Strategy

Standing on the verge of the twentieth century, Gustav Mahler (1860–1911) reinvented the classical symphony and radically updated it for our times. Mahler was truly a big thinker, creating his own style rather than following established rules. The American conductor and composer Leonard Bernstein once called Mahler's music "the utterance of a genius, an authentic original . . . it is a treasure trove of originality."[5]

I became interested in Mahler on Thursday, January 31, 2002, when I tuned in to my favorite classical music radio station, WQXR, and listened to the ending of a live performance of the Third Symphony, conducted by Mariss Jansons with the New York Philharmonic. The children's choir of the sixth movement ("Es sungen drei Engel") was playing as I tuned in, and then, there it was: the sublime Adagio in D major, titled *Langsam, Ruhevoll, Empfunden* (slowly, tranquilly, deeply felt). Soon I manically started to attend Mahler symphony performances—the Third, then the Fifth, the First, the Second, and the marvelous Sixth (see "Mahler's Sixth Symphony").[6]

In an important essay, musicologist Edward Reilly analyzed how Mahler went through the process of creating his symphonies through a series of sketches.[7] The process included:

Mahler's Sixth Symphony (composer's original score).

Source: Music Division, The New York Public Library for the Performing Arts, Astor, Lenox and Tildon Foundations.

"first ideas for the work," "preliminary sketches, exploring the possibilities of developing and combining different themes and motifs," "preliminary drafts in which the basic sequence for a full movement . . . is laid out," "draft full scores . . . in which the instrumentation in one or more movements is worked out," and then, the "final autograph full score," although Mahler still made significant modifications each time after the work was performed. Mahler treated a musical score as a lively and dynamic document that elaborates his initial ideas, combines and synthesizes them, and puts them into a sequence.

The result: highly original symphonic music.

Mahler used massive orchestras and choruses (a total of 1,028 performers took part in the first performance of his Eighth Symphony), yet he often achieved a chamber music–like intimacy in many of his symphonies. Mahler quoted—and then deconstructed—waltzes, ländlers, and military marches. Most important, he did not follow the classical tradition of four clearly defined movements (the first was quick, the second was slow, the third was in a three-part structure, and the fourth was quick again). Instead, Mahler's symphonies comprised as few as two movements—or as many as eight. He included songs in his symphonies; he even ended one with a song (the Second).

You can develop your strategy score in a similar way. Like Mahler, use elaboration, synthesis and sequence to flesh out your strategy. View your strategy score as a lively and dynamic document. Don't squeeze your insights into a cookie-cutter format. Mahler did not squeeze his original ideas into the typical four-movement symphony scheme either.

So I ask myself, whenever I sit in a strategy meeting where a sprawling set of creative business ideas must be given form and shape to become a strategy score, What would Mahler do?

Mahler was not alone. Other composers use similar techniques, even when they compose different kinds of music. David Rogers is a contemporary New York composer whose music synthesizes African and jazz elements. He recently arranged African xylophone music for an orchestra at Carnegie Hall. So I asked him how he builds a musical strategy out of these different elements. "My pieces usually start with a couple different ideas; they may come from different musical styles, like jazz and African fiddle music. In composing, I take each idea and elaborate on it, expanding it into new directions. Then I explore how the different ideas can be combined or play off each other. Once I have those elaborations and possible combinations, I start to build a dramatic sequence in time, an arc that will allow the piece to unfold."

Google's strategy over the last few years can be viewed as a systematic unfolding of a strategy score. Google's original big idea was quite simple: to concentrate entirely on search in a way that other competitors had not. But elaborating on that idea led to different elements that the company had to plan for: What would the algorithm be (to make sure search results were great)? What would the interface be like (to make sure it was easy and intuitive for users)? What would the advertising mechanism be (to make sure it generated revenue)? Some of these elements needed to be synthesized or combined—for example, advertising had to work with the user interface in such a way that the users knew what was a sponsored listing, so that they maintained trust in the validity of search results. And as Google's strategy was built, a sequence was needed to roll out each stage of its search capacity: first text search, then images, then maps, and later (as usage rose) blog and video searches.

Or consider Lotte Corporation, a widely diversified Korean *chaebol*, which decided to enter the Chinese market. For a big market like China that is quickly becoming crowded with multinationals, you need a Big Think strategy. For Lotte, the key issues were: Which businesses should we take to China? How should we localize these businesses and their product lines to create value for Chinese consumers? Who should be our partners? Which businesses or product lines should we combine to leverage resources? How should we sequence the entry into the Chinese market? To address these issues, the company designed a strategy score that was communicated to Chinese customers in an original corporate advertisement, featuring a conductor and Lotte's various businesses.

From Strategy Score to Execution

Once we have a strategy score, we are ready for execution, and execution cannot be taken lightly. A bad performance can ruin the best strategy. Early strategy literature was entirely focused on strategy formulation, and it neglected execution entirely. But many strategies fail because there isn't enough attention to execution.[8]

Lotte ad campaign for China

Source: LOTTE Co., Ltd.

To begin with, of course, you need a budget for the execution of your strategy. A Big Think project must be sufficiently funded. There must be close attention to cost, and to investments required for spearheading the project. There also must be a clear understanding of how much customers are willing to pay; that is, pricing must be value based, not just cost based. It must be clear how Big Think will make money.

But there is much more to execution than budgeting and financial projections. The strategy must be translated into an operational plan. This includes defining specific objectives and timelines, assigning people to projects, and, most important, getting everybody pumped up for executing the Big Think.

Again, there is a similarity to a symphony because a great composition still hinges on a great performance. To achieve success and lasting impact, you must master both roles. Gustav Mahler was not only a great composer but also a great orchestra conductor, of both his own work and that of others. You, too, must be not only a composer of the strategy but also the conductor of the work when you execute it. The best composition can fall apart in the hands of an inept conductor, just as the best strategy can fail if it is not executed in the right way.

-5-

Executing
Big Think

How to Pull the Ship
over the Mountain

ORMULATING A STRATEGY is very important in Big
Think, but it is not enough to win. Chinese philosopher
Sun Tzu's dictum that "every battle is won before it is ever
fought" must be complemented by U.S. boxer Mike Tyson's
alleged punch line, "Everybody has a plan, until they get hit in
the face."[1]

Great strategy hinges ultimately on its execution. Think of
Odysseus's plan to use the Trojan horse. It was a brilliant plan
to sneak inside the walled city and open its gates after ten years
of fruitless siege warfare. But its success relied on a host of factors that were all about the execution. To start, Odysseus

needed a team with diverse skills: the carpenter Epeius to build the horse; the spy Sinon, who presented the false gift to the enemy; and—bravest of all—the soldiers who would fill the belly of the beast and risk their lives behind enemy lines. Epeius's horse was a masterpiece of design. Sinon succeeded in tricking the Trojans into accepting the gift horse into their city. That night, Odysseus's crew opened the horse's secret door. At that point, they had only a matter of seconds to accomplish their mission of opening the gates before the guards were alerted. The strategic gamble paid off. Troy was conquered overnight, and the poets (Homer and Virgil) made Odysseus's masterstroke famous for the ages.

Executing a Big Think strategy is different from implementing a more traditional strategy. It is at the same time more challenging and demanding, and more exciting and rewarding. You are in untested territory, but you can make a big difference. You run the risk of failing, but you may also become the envy of the entire industry. You may get hit in the face, or you may walk away as a hero with just a few scratches.

Big Think execution is a sprint. There are many hurdles that you must jump over before you reach the finish line of business success. The first hurdle is to overcome inertia and resistance among your employees and create enthusiasm and sufficient commitment for the strategy. Your employees should not just buy in; you must tap into their aspirations and dreams. The second hurdle is to roll out the strategy successfully over time. Big Think strategy does not hang on the wall like a beautiful canvas; it is a dynamic document laying out creative ideas in detail and in sequence like a musical score. As part of the execution, you must specify milestones and plan for quick wins.

Another hurdle you will face is environmental changes. You must adjust your execution accordingly: there is not enough time to align the entire organization perfectly; instead, be flexible in organizing teams and structures. The final hurdle is to get people outside the organization excited about your Big Think. For that to happen, you must cause a big splash in the marketplace.

Fitzcarraldo: Executing the Impossible

"Werner Herzog's *Fitzcarraldo* is a movie in the great tradition of grandiose cinematic visions," writes movie critic Roger Ebert.[2] It is also a testament to determination, obsession, and the madness that is needed to execute the impossible.

Brian Sweeney Fitzgerald (called "Fitzcarraldo") is a businessman and an obsessive music lover who wants to build an opera house in the rain forest. To get the money for his venture, he plans to make a fortune in the rubber business by exploiting untapped rubber trees up the Pongo River. To get to the Pongo, he must drag his steamship from the Amazon River, up a mountain, and then down to the Pongo. It is the sheer madness of this idea—and its cinematic realization—that explains the cult status of the movie.

The real-life Fitzcarraldo is the filmmaker himself, Werner Herzog, a man obsessed with the ambition of executing the grand scheme of the film—and the critical scene of pulling the ship over a mountain—realistically. For the climactic scene of the movie, Herzog hired local Peruvians to haul the enormous ship—inch by inch, with a real block and pulley system— across a real mountain. Herzog used no ship models or special

Klaus Kinski as Fitzcarraldo

Photo Fitzcarraldo
© Werner Herzog Film.
Used with permission.

effects because he knew this would compromise his vision. He demanded truth.

The making of the movie near Iquitos in Peru, five hundred miles away from any major city, was an ordeal. Herzog had to change the location because a border war broke out between Peru and Ecuador. He then shot for four months with Jason Robards as Fitzcarraldo and Mick Jagger playing Fitzcarraldo's assistant. But Robards fell ill, and Jagger toured with the Rolling Stones instead. Herzog decided to start all over again. He turned to Klaus Kinski, an actor known for his temperamental fluctuations.

Herzog had worked with Kinski before, so he should have known what he was getting into. As might be expected, Kinski behaved badly on the set and did not get along with the locals. Managing his daily tantrums occupied most of Herzog's time. One of the natives offered to kill Kinski for him, but Herzog declined because he needed him to finish the filming.

"*Fitzcarraldo* is not a perfect movie," writes movie critic Ebert. "But as a document of a quest and a dream, and as the record of man's audacity and foolish, visionary heroism, there has never been another movie like it."[3]

Tap into Their Dreams

To execute a really bold project, you need a driven and passionate project manager. Somebody who will fully commit to the project and turn it into a life mission. Somebody who will pull the ship over the mountain.

At one point, when the *Fitzcarraldo* project seemed to be stalling, investors asked Herzog whether he would like to quit. "If I abandon this project, I will be a man without dreams," he replied. "I live my life or I end my life with this project."[4]

Like the project manager, team members must be invested with their minds and hearts. The project manager must tap into the aspirations and dreams of every individual team member. I am not talking about buy-in here. Buy-in is a manipulative command-and-control system, and everyone sees right through it. Think of how a corporate buy-in process usually works. At the beginning of the strategic planning process, senior leaders select the few heads that they believe are favorable to what they intend to do. This leadership team then designs the strategy without much input from others. The buy-in then occurs top down through the corporate hierarchy via motivational speeches, strategy papers, e-mails, meetings, and workshops. Individual employees, who are supposed to execute the strategy in the field, are informed about why the strategy is needed and what it entails, but they do not see the benefit and thus cannot make the strategy their own. Because there is nothing in it for them, their buy-in will be forced. Lack of motivation will be the outcome.

In contrast, Big Think execution requires that people perform with enthusiasm. We need not motivate *them*, they motivate *themselves.* In line with the Big Think strategy, employees will set their own individual goals, striving to achieve their career and personal dreams. They will see the project as a means to their own growth. In other words, we instill some sense of higher calling. People are devoted to the strategy because they are able to "self-actualize," in a Maslowian sense, when they execute the Big Think strategy.

For all of that to happen, the Big Think strategy must be inspirational. It must be a positive force in people's lives and be given a high priority within the organization. The professional and personal rewards to each employee must be clearly communicated. Leaders must talk to employees, look them in the eye, and listen to their dreams.

When they do, magic things happen. Employees feel understood, motivated, and connected to the mission. When I spoke at an annual leadership event at Liz Claiborne about this sort of inspirational leadership, one of the participants, working for Lucky Brand, spontaneously gave a pep talk to the entire group about how excited she is every day to get to work.

Plan for Milestones and Quick Wins

Big Think success rarely happens overnight. It takes time. It takes time to get ready for execution, to launch, and to roll out. It takes time for customers to overcome their reservations, to get used to the new idea, and to see how it is valuable to them. It takes time to gain distribution in a new market. It may take a few weeks, months, or a couple of years before you can see results.

One of my Asian clients set precise milestones for its entry into the U.S. market. The first milestone was to establish a flagship retail store to attract the attention of consumers and department stores. The next milestone was to have a counter in a prominent department store with nationwide presence, in a key city. The milestone after that was to get limited distribution within the department store chain, and so on. The execution toward each goal made it necessary to plan new product introductions as well as related PR and media events accordingly.

In addition, you need quick wins early on. Few employees will be excited throughout the process and patiently strive for full market domination. Skepticism may kick in. Was it such a good idea after all? If the Big Think idea does not seem likely to deliver, some will prefer to coast or just jump ship.

For example, consider a radically new product that is supposed to target a new market. For that situation, it is appropriate to set milestones for specific markets and along the diffusion-of-innovation curve. A quick win may be achieved by capturing a test market. The market may then still be small, but everyone will see that there is potential. The next milestone could be gaining awareness among the innovative users of the total market. After that early success, the Big Think operational plan should focus on broader market acceptance, and there must be a success yardstick for that.

The Absolut vodka market entry into the United States in the early 1980s followed this approach. Supported by a cool advertising campaign depicting the shape of the bottle, Absolut quickly won over Bostonians and New Yorkers. It then expanded to other East Coast cities, always targeting trendy bars, then entered the West Coast, and finally national distribution. Absolut has been the best-selling imported vodka in the United States for years.

Quick wins are critical to buy time. They create an aura of success. They can give you a break and take you out from under the magnifying glass for a while as you prepare your next steps. Also, as every good fund-raiser knows, announce the campaign only when you already have a substantial amount of money in your pocket. Similarly, only announce your milestones once they are safe bets.

Organize Flexibly

When you are launching a Big Think project, competitors will respond, customer preferences and trends will change, and soon your Big Think will not seem so big any more. Organizational leaders often fixate on "aligning the entire organization" perfectly around a new strategy. Frankly, in Big Think, you do not have time for that.

Neither does a coach in football (or, as it is called in the United States, soccer). Before the game, the coach puts together a strategy and assembles the team of players. As the game unfolds, the coach must flexibly reorganize the team. During halftime, the coach, with input from the team, decides on how the strategy should be executed after halftime. Depending on the score, the coach may ask players to take on new positions; he or she may ask them to play more defensively or offensively; if necessary, some players will be exchanged. The coach must make these decisions with the project goal in mind—for example, to win the game, or to win by a certain number of points to qualify for the next round; or to reach a tie, and so on. The game is not the right moment for major structural changes; there is no time for extensive personnel debates. Many players will be the same for the entire game, but you can make a difference by flexibly reorganizing.

Like football coaches, businesses leaders must be prepared to reorganize their teams flexibly as well. Big Think projects are inherently cross-functional. To execute a Big Think project, a leader must organize the team into cross-functional units that perform interrelated tasks oriented toward one common goal: to execute the strategy efficiently and effectively. Moreover, everybody must support everybody else and be willing to take on another task if so required. Some team members will need to shift positions midway through a project. Spontaneous reorganization is a fact of life: it occurs at the molecular level of the brain, where brain cells or neurons can take on functions that they were originally not designed for, as well as at the macro level of groups.

Make a Big Splash

Finally, to execute a Big Think strategy successfully, you must make a big splash in the market. To ensure that happens, you must identify what captures everybody's attention and imagination and use bold communications. On the way, if you are clever, you may get a little help from your friends—the customers.

Find the Attention Getters

Dubai, part of the United Arab Emirates, is engaged in a massive economic development program that aims to liberate its economy from dependence on oil (reserves are projected to run out by 2010) by making the country a hub for global service industries such as IT, finance, and media as well as a destination for tourism. The strategy has been hugely successful, with oil now accounting for only 6 percent of GDP.

As part of the execution, Dubai has not just been building ports and free-trade business zones in its unprecedented program of real estate development. Dubai has also launched several projects that are drawing the world's attention to this tiny Arab emirate. One attention getter is the Burj Al Arab—a dramatic "seven-star" hotel on the coast. Every room is a lavish suite. You arrive by Rolls-Royce limousine, helicopter, or submarine. Another development, Palm Dubai, is a complex of hundreds of luxury villas, the largest land reclamation project ever and one of the few man-made structures that is visible from outer space. More than that, Dubai hosts one of the world's largest artificial skiing resorts, in the middle of a desert. It is also constructing some of the largest buildings on earth. When I visited recently, I learned that Dubai's leaders are thinking about creating attention getters at all levels. Tourism is one part of the new economic mix for the country, but it is also a way of getting the business world to visit and discover that it can now open global operations in this Middle East state. With all its

The seven-star Burj Al Arab Hotel

Source: fotosearch.com.

buzz, Dubai has been successfully stealing attention away from other city-states like Singapore.

Singapore has noticed. When Chin Nam Tan, permanent secretary of the Ministry of Information, Communications and the Arts, heard that I was writing a book on "Big Think strategy," he invited me to give a seminar for his staff and hold a breakfast meeting with members of the Singapore government. Like Dubai, Singapore is always committed to upgrading its infrastructure and economic competitiveness and making it more attractive for investors, tourists, and talents. Over the last few years, Singapore has significantly enhanced its infrastructure and gained attention through cultural and entertainment facilities and events, adding excitement to a place that visitors had before found beautiful but quite boring. I love Big Think competition among city-states!

Use Bold Communications

In addition to attention getters, bold communications are part of creating a big splash. Think of the great advertising campaigns: Nike's "Just Do It," the Marlboro Man, Avis's "We Try Harder," De Beers's "A Diamond Is Forever," or the Absolut bottle print ads. (I am sure you have your own list; these ads are on the *Advertising Age* top ten ad list of all time.) They are still conversation pieces today. They have reached cult status.

However, do not just think advertising. Web sites, new media, even sponsorships can be part of big-splash executions. Yet, often they are not employed to their fullest potential. Many sponsorships, for example, are just banner campaigns—you put up your company logo on a banner over the stage, and you are done.

"At Audi, we use sponsorship to upgrade the image and prestige of our brand to become the most successful maker of prestige cars," Ralph Weyler, chief marketing officer of Audi, told me. "A sponsorship must have impact. It must be part of a total package." During the course of writing this book, I had the chance to experience Audi sponsorship activities firsthand during the Salzburg Opera Festival, the Hahnenkamm ski race in Kitzbühel, Austria, and in Las Vegas. At each of these venues, and at others, Audi offers a complete package, including entertainment of VIP guests, an Audi-driving experience, and limousine service (in Las Vegas, forty brand-new R8 sports cars were all cruising, one after the other, along the Strip). This creates much more customer buzz than any banner placed in a sports arena.

Finally, communications must be integrated to have maximum impact. Take Dove's Campaign for Real Beauty. The campaign began with a big idea, based on research that indi-

The Audi R8 experience

Source: AUDI AG. Used with permission.

cated that women around the world were tired of the beauty stereotypes used in advertising. To convey the big idea that beauty comes in many forms, an integrated communications campaign was created to connect with women worldwide on many levels.

The campaign started with a Web site. Then Dove's ad agency, Ogilvy & Mather, launched a series of outdoor and print ads featuring "real women" with real curves, full figures, gray hair, and freckles. Several billboards featured an interactive element that let viewers vote on whether a woman was "fat or fab," "wrinkled or wonderful," "gray or gorgeous," or "flawed or flawless" through text messaging. In one week, over half a million people had cast a vote for the billboard on Times Square in New York. All communications were designed to get people talking and create a buzz. In addition, Dove partnered with the *Oprah Winfrey Show*, where the campaign was featured during the first week of the U.S. launch.

"The power behind Dove's Campaign for Real Beauty comes not only from the idea itself, but also from the integrated communications behind it. There was a huge PR component in the campaign launch. There's an interactive Web site where women can talk to each other and exchange views. Dove even set up a fund for young women to help communicate to them that beauty can be many different things," says Shelly Lazarus, chairman and CEO of Ogilvy and Mather Worldwide. The free publicity Dove received from U.S. media coverage of the campaign as of mid-2006 has been estimated to exceed $21 million.[5]

Get Help from Customers

As you roll out your Big Think strategy, do not keep everything hidden within the organization. Involve people outside the organization. Consider craigslist.

Craigslist.org is a simple Web site helping people with everyday needs, such as finding a job or a place to live, through classified ads. Craigslist's key source of revenues is job ads (about US$25 per ad in New York). In spring 2007, craigslist.org featured 450 cities in 50 countries and served over 6 billion page views per month, putting it in eighth place among Web sites based in the United States. Craigslist does not use any form of traditional marketing. In fact, the entire Web site is largely run by users. This keeps the company lean (at the beginning of 2007, it had twenty-three employees) and focused on customer service. "It happened organically. It happened without conscious intent on our part," Craig Newmark, founder of craigslist.org, told me. "You provide a trustworthy environment. You give people a break. You make it easy for people to give you a break. That seems to work."

Similarly, a tremendous big splash during the 2006 FIFA World Cup, which involved customers, was the so-called fan fests, designated areas equipped with huge screens and speakers, allowing football fans from all countries to gather and watch the games. The fan fests transformed the fan experience and turned the World Cup into a huge party. This innovative idea, conceived by Schmidt und Kaiser, an event agency, is likely to be repeated globally during the 2010 games.

Over the Mountain, into the Rainbow

You have cleared the four hurdles of Big Think execution now. You have tapped into the dreams of your employees. You have planned for milestones and quick wins. You have set up flexible organizational structures that have rapidly responded to a changing environment. You have grabbed everyone's attention.

You have made it. You *have* pulled the ship over the mountain—and into the rainbow.

How does it feel?

SHANGHAI, CHINA

I am riding on the magnetic levitation train, the Maglev, from the international airport to Pudong. Top speed: 431 kmh, or 268 mph. Total travel time for the 30-kilometer (18.6-mile) ride: 7 minutes and 20 seconds. Hardly enough time to start proofreading my new book.

My mind drifts off. "What Big Think have I done myself? Herzog pulled a ship over a mountain. Mahler revolutionized symphonies. Sure, I wrote this book. But it contains the ideas and tools that others will use. What have I actually done for myself? *Was habe ich denn schon gebaut?*"

And then it hits me. "I have not fulfilled my calling and built the Trojan horse."

I get off the train. I rush to the escalator down to the street level and grab a taxi, getting seated in the back.

I type frantically into my handheld translator and show the screen to my taxi driver:

"请带我去巨鹿路153号." (Take me to 153 Julu Road.)

"Why go there? Only fashion shop near there at Chang Le Road."

I type my reply: "没关系, 带我去, 我有任务要完成. 我必须建立电脑程式**内**的病毒." (Never mind. Just take me there. I have to fulfill a mission. I have to build the Trojan horse.)

He seems confused. "建立病毒？... 什么乱七八糟的？ ... 不懂 ... 这老外是不是有毛病啊？先到了再说吧 ..." (Trojan Horse?!! What is this all about? So confusing... What's wrong with this foreigner? Anyway, let's go there first. . .)

-6-

Leading Big Think

Guts, Passion—or Just a Robot?

SHOULD WE REPLACE executives with robots?

I am not asking this question to be facetious. Robots and computers that solve complex problems are turning up everywhere. Millions of workers have already been replaced by robots in manufacturing. Humanoid robots are now appearing at Universal Studios and Disney. Computers are replacing fund managers. Deep Blue, an IBM computer, won a six-game chess match against Garry Kasparov, the reigning world chess champion, now retired.

So, could we improve the quality of business decision making and leadership with some form of artificial intelligence? Or is there a very special, inimitably human skill that executives bring to leading and managing, and is that skill needed to launch big and bold corporate initiatives?

Eliza and Jack

Let me address this sensitive topic first indirectly. "Eliza" is a 1966 computer program written by Joseph Weizenbaum that mimics—in fact, parodies—Carl Rogers's person-centered psychotherapy. In Rogerian therapy, a therapist encourages a patient to explore his or her feelings by listening and then mirroring back what the patient revealed. Here is a typical conversation, slightly shortened from Weizenbaum's original paper:[1]

Patient: Men are all alike.

Eliza: In what way?

Patient: They're always bugging us about something or other.

Eliza: Can you think of a specific example?

Patient: Well, my boyfriend made me come here.

Eliza: Your boyfriend made you come here?

Patient: He says I'm depressed much of the time.

Eliza: I am sorry to hear you are depressed.

Patient: It is true. I am unhappy.

Eliza: Do you think coming here will help you not to be unhappy?

Patient: I need some help, that much seems certain.

Eliza: What would it mean to you if you got some help?

Patient: Perhaps I could learn to get along with my mother.

Eliza: Tell me more about your family.

Patient: My father is afraid of everybody.

Eliza: What else comes to your mind when you think of your father?

Patient: Bullies.

Eliza: Does that have anything to do with the fact that your boyfriend made you come here?

Doesn't it sound amazingly realistic? You can try out Eliza on your own vexing questions: Java versions of the program are widely available on the Internet. Which raises the question: if a computer program can fake a therapist, could it also fake a CEO? Could we write a program (call it "Jack") that could replicate the following typical management conversation?

Regional manager: Hi, Jack.

Jack: So, Fred, have you hit your quarterly numbers?

Regional manager: We're a little low. But we have a plan to fix it.

Jack: Did you check it with legal?

Regional manager: Of course.

Jack: Did you show the numbers to the CFO?

Regional manager: Yes.

Jack: Is it aligned with our corporate vision?

Regional manager: Yes. And I think this plan will impress the investors.

Jack: How will this impact my bonus?

Regional manager: Well, I think there is a real opportunity to make some waves here. We must execute against the plan.

Jack: Cut costs.

Regional manager: We have tried, but that is raising some quality issues.

Jack: Have you implemented Six Sigma?

Regional manager: Of course.

Jack: Are you number one or number two in your business category?

Regional manager: Actually, no. No, we're not.

Jack: Fire 10 percent of your staff.

Regional manager: Uh . . . yes, we have. As you requested.

Jack: Great. I will see you on Saturday 7:00 a.m. on the golf course. Bring sunscreen.

Of course, we could write a program that mimics a CEO conversation. However, our programmed CEO "Jack," like

Robot CEO

Source: fotosearch.com.

therapist "Eliza," understands nothing. Both simply run on simple natural-language programs. Eliza rephrases statements into questions and turns key words into canned phrases to give the appearance of understanding. Jack responds to the word *plan* with "cut costs," associates any semantic phrase related to *quality* with "Six Sigma," and is prompted by grammatical negation to make a command to fire people.

In the late 1970s, Eliza and similar programs were enthusiastically embraced by the artificial intelligence community as the dawn of a new age. Several decades later, with computers and robots much more sophisticated and millions of times faster, we still do not have a single program that has passed the Turing test. This test, conceived in 1950 by Alan Turing, an

English mathematician who is considered the father of computer science, proposes that a human judge engages in a text conversation with two parties—one human and one machine—about haircuts, for example (Turing's idea of a conversation topic, not mine).[2] If the judge cannot reliably discern which is which, the machine is said to pass the test. But after nearly sixty years, no computer has ever succeeded in fooling the judge in the Turing test.

It seems that the human brain is somewhat different from a machine.

How Humans Differ from Robots

By now, the consensus is as follows: computers are great at performing repetitive tasks in well-defined and well-controlled worlds—be it complex mathematics, car assembly, chess, or linguistic tasks. However, computers are really bad at dealing with what is called "commonsense knowledge."

Creative tasks, like Big Think problems, require exactly this kind of knowledge, which includes reasoning by analogy, seeing unusual connections, and elaborating on a problem from different angles—not to mention self-motivating skills and motivating others. In fact, Eliza and other early programs were so successful precisely because they sidestepped the problem of giving the program a database of real-world knowledge.

More than that, in approaching their tasks, some humans bring certain attitudes and motivational states that are impossible to simulate in a machine. Individuals can be confident that they will find a solution and risk everything to find it—no matter what. They have guts. While they engage in a task, they are not just following a routine (or subroutine); they truly love solving the task, and they do it with passion. Finally, they do not easily give up and crash, like a computer, when they cannot find a solution immediately. They change their approach and show perseverance. At least some people do, and it turns out those are the leaders who drive Big Think.

Leadership: The Elusive Topic

Leadership is one of the perennial topics of management. A lot has been written on leadership—about types of leadership and leadership styles, about qualities of leadership and support structures, about leaders and followers, and about leadership development.

When I think of visionary leaders of the past, I think of Odysseus, who conceived the Trojan horse as a strategy to penetrate Troy. Brilliant out-of-the-box thinking. Not only that: it took tremendous leadership to pull it off. How would you convince a dozen soldiers to climb inside a wooden horse and be delivered to the enemy as a gift? Odysseus was a great communicator who knew how to set an agenda and focus his team on the big idea at the core of their strategy. By contrast, think of Agamemnon, the Greek army's titular leader who had led them to ten years of battlefield stalemate. Agamemnon could have easily been replaced by a computer program like Jack.

After Troy fell, Odysseus led his ship on a voyage home that proved fraught with peril. His leadership on the voyage formed the basis of his most legendary tale: *The Odyssey* by Homer. As a leader, Odysseus displays great courage in the face of antagonists like the one-eyed giant Cyclops and the six-headed monster Scylla. He perseveres despite countless trials and obstacles: the dope-peddling Lotus Eaters, the appetites of the Laestrygonian cannibals, and the magical charms of the enchantress Circe. Through the long ordeal, Odysseus is driven by the desire to save his men, to return home to Ithaca, and to reunite with his beloved wife, Penelope, after seventeen long years of separation.

So is there a recipe for leadership that we can draw from Homer's epic? What are the traits and behaviors associated with a leader who challenges the status quo, engages in bold new ventures, and pulls others along in doing so?

The Big Three of Big Think

In 1994, two management professors, Robert House of the Wharton School and Philip Podsakoff of Indiana University, did a comprehensive review of research on leadership to identify the behaviors of outstanding leaders.[3] Many of the leadership styles that they identified apply to any kind of leadership—such as articulating a vision, acting as role models, and communicating expectations. These styles are not unimportant for Big Think; however, they are not specific to it. Yet, a few are highly relevant for Big Think leadership, and they are exactly those traits and behaviors that computing machines are bad at: confidence and determination, passion, and persistence—or what I call "the big three of Big Think": guts, passion, and perseverance.

Guts

Big Think leadership takes courage and nerve—in a word, guts. Guts is the opposite of comfortably settling in with the status quo, giving in to others, and muddling through by keeping things vague and not letting yourself and your projects be judged.

Many leaders may be effective at managing the status quo. They are not bad leaders: they articulate a vision, they act as role models, they clearly communicate expectations. But they lack the guts to think big.

Guts is not about pushing your will onto others and not giving a damn. Guts is not being brusque or impatient or having a bad temper. Guts is really about values, commitment, and responsibility.

Guts means having the energy to challenge long-held beliefs. It takes guts to enter an engineering-driven company and argue for a customer perspective. That is what Marty Homlish did when he was hired as chief marketing officer of enterprise software company SAP in 2000. He had just finished a stint at Sony launching the PlayStation and the compact disc. Upon his arrival, Homlish found a company where everyone spoke what he dubbed "SAPanese." The B2B firm was so entrenched in its engineering culture that it had never learned to talk to customers, to explain its complex products, or to communicate its fundamental value proposition to its clients' top management. But Homlish was thrilled by the challenge. "I knew SAP was a marketer's dream: we already had great products, a strong history of innovation, and a loyal customer base—all we needed to do was transform marketing." In a few short years, he formed a new SAP Global Marketing company and drove home a powerful and consistent message about the SAP brand. He led an organizational realignment of the whole company, from an engineering and product focus to a market and customer focus. The results were plain to see: in five years, the estimated value of the SAP brand (according to the Inter-brand/*BusinessWeek* annual rankings) rose $2.86 billion, or 46 percent.[4]

Guts means sticking with your view against pressure from others. This is not easy at all. Consider the pressure to con-form and obey commands demonstrated in a series of classic social psychology experiments done in the 1960s and 1970s. In one experiment, participants were shown several lines on a board and asked which one was the longest.[5] The task was quite easy; however, confederates in the room consistently re-ported the wrong line. About one-third of participants con-formed to the erroneous majority view of the others in the room. In another experiment, participants were directed by the experiment to administer what they thought were electro-shocks of increasing voltages to another person.[6] Two-thirds of participants went all the way to (what they believed to be) 450 volts. Fortunately, at times, people also stand up against others, even risking their lives. It happens in totalitarian regimes and wars, and it has been shown in another series of social psychology experiments. This sort of "minority influence," acting according to what one feels is right, can be a role model for others, and therefore powerful leadership behavior.[7] It is critical for Big Think, where you often have to go against the mainstream. You need guts to use out-of-the-box idea-sourcing techniques. You need guts to argue for bold ideas during an evaluation process. You need guts to execute them without watering them down to make them acceptable to everybody. You also need guts to implement the organizational changes they may require.

Guts means defining standards that you can be judged against, making those standards public, and sticking to them, no matter what. In the extreme, guts can mean putting yourself, your job, your reputation on the line. When you have guts, you make yourself accountable. You invite feedback from your direct reports—the people who work for you, not just your boss. You ask them about how effective you are and what they would do if they were you. You may not like what you hear, but you have the guts to ask and then act on it.

When Carlos Ghosn became the COO of Nissan in October 1999, he promised that the company would turn a profit in 2000 or he and the rest of the executive committee would quit.[8] This was a bold statement, considering that the company was $20 billion in debt. Ghosn lived up to his promise and went on to become Nissan's president in June 2000 and was named chief executive officer in June 2001. Although Ghosn was an outsider who challenged Nissan's culture, cut staff and suppliers, and made executives accountable for results, he has become a celebrity figure in Japan. The guts he showed in the turnaround of Nissan have earned him respect worldwide for his management skills.

Ultimately, guts means having the courage to overcome your fears and put your anxieties in perspective—whether they are fears of failure, fears of losing, or fears of embarrassing yourself. You must address your fears and take actions that get you to your goal or desired outcome.

Passion

The second of the big three of Big Think is passion. Big Think leaders are passionate about their strategy. Not only do they believe in their visionary strategy, they go out of their way to convince and motivate others. They feel passionate and enthusiastic about their Big Think and want others to know.

Passion is a strong emotion. Strong emotions are usually associated with private life more than work. With people we are close to rather than those with whom we have a formal relationship. With hobbies rather than occupations. With something we choose to do rather than with tasks that are chosen for and assigned to us.

Big Think leaders apply these same emotions to projects and people at work—to their "Big Think baby." In fact, the distinction between work and nonwork makes little sense to them.

Passion was what drove Commissioner David Stern to revive the nearly moribund National Basketball Association (NBA) in the early 1980s. When he assumed the league's top job in 1984, the NBA was being torn apart by player drug scandals and labor battles between team owners and athletes. Fans were dropping off in worrisome numbers, and dwindling arena crowds meant plummeting revenues and a league edging toward bankruptcy.

Stern had a love for the game since his childhood. As he recently told an audience at Columbia Business School, those boyhood dreams remained vibrant in his head and heart as an adult. He remembered paying 50 cents to attend games—the ticket price for a New York school kid. "I was hooked," he said, smiling.

From the beginning, Stern thought big about instilling—or perhaps reinvigorating—a sense of pride in the game from within the league itself, something he felt it had lost somewhere along the way. He built the framework for big marketing deals, pushed for new arenas, and helped the NBA ink contracts with TV networks that would send more cash flowing back into the teams, perpetuating the health of the league as its audience expanded into millions of living rooms. By 2000, annual revenue in the NBA had increased more than five-fold during his tenure. He has been widely lauded for instituting hard-line punishment against player drug abuse. Stern's passion for the game led him to become one of sports' most effective corporate executives.

Perseverance

The last of the big three of the Big Think is perseverance. Perseverance is about endurance, from idea sourcing to evaluation, strategy formulation, and implementation. Perseverance means sticking to it when resistance arises, when failure looms. Not giving up when it gets hard.

In January 2005, Nicholas Negroponte, director of the MIT Media Lab, announced the One Laptop Per Child (OLPC) initiative, a program to produce $100 laptops for the world's poorest children. This would be a bold announcement to make at any venue, but Negroponte chose to make it in front of world leaders at the World Economic Forum in Davos, Switzerland.

Despite criticism by skeptics who question Negroponte's approach, and huge obstacles in designing and manufacturing $100 laptops by the millions, he has held firm to his goal of changing the way children learn. Negroponte envisions the laptops to be "a window into the world and a tool with which to think."[9] While many critics believe the money would be better spent by building schools or providing more textbooks, Negroponte believes the computers can help children "learn learning" even if they lack an opportunity to attend a traditional school.

Another challenge almost as big as changing the way children learn is producing a computer that can be sold for $100. The first challenge was to design a useful computer that is able to connect wirelessly from remote locations and function in areas where there is no available electricity. The OLPC team has gone through several designs, including a model that featured a hand crank for power. To meet its pricing goal, OLPC will produce the machines in mass quantity—only selling the machines to government agencies that place an order for 1 million or more computers.

At first, even big thinkers like Steve Jobs of Apple dismissed the project as a "science experiment," but he has since contributed his own ideas to the project. Bill Gates has been critical of the fact that the laptops will run on UNIX instead of the Windows platform. He has also challenged the idea of using laptops, saying the goals would be better met by using handheld computers with mobile phone technology.

Through hard work and perseverance, and the financial support of companies and individuals including Google, Nortel, Advanced Micro Devices (AMD), and Rupert Murdoch, Negroponte is moving closer to realizing his vision. OLPC unveiled a working prototype of the laptop in summer 2006 with an estimated cost of $135 per unit. As distribution becomes larger, Negroponte's team hopes to hit the magic $100 mark in the near future and plans to ship 10 million machines in 2007.

Negroponte's commitment and perseverance were summed up in a November 2005 interview in *Fortune* magazine when he was asked about the prospect of the project's failing. "Failure means it's $142.07 and six months late. Failure doesn't mean it doesn't happen or it's a bad idea," said Negroponte.[10]

Have an Agenda

NEW YORK CITY

I am sitting in a TV studio preparing to be interviewed by Dharshini David for *BBC World* about a memorandum written by Chairman Howard Schultz to his senior managers at Starbucks, which has been leaked to the press.

The memo is lying in my lap. "Subject: The Commoditization of the Starbucks Experience." In the memo, Schultz talks about the "watering down" and "dilution" of the experience that led to the "commoditization" of the Starbucks brand. Sure, Starbucks has achieved immense "growth, development and scale" but at what cost?

"This is quite an extraordinary memo," I say to myself. "This guy has guts. This guy thinks big. He has an agenda."

"Ready, Professor Schmitt?"

I skim the rest of the memo: "I take full responsibility myself," "I have said for 20 years that our success is not an entitlement," "let us get back to the core," "push for innovation," "once again differentiate Starbucks from all the others."

"Five seconds to go, Professor Schmitt. Four, three, two . . ."

Big Think leadership is not all about personality traits. It also helps to approach tasks a certain way—for example, to have an agenda.

Big Think leaders are quite open about their agenda. They feel they can't waste time. They can lay out their agenda for you, and they will make it clear that they are not willing to compromise.

Dov Charney, like Howard Schultz, has an agenda. While the rest of the world has gone global in apparel manufacturing, the outspoken founder of American Apparel has stuck to U.S. soil, cutting and sewing every cotton hoodie, sweatpant, and T-shirt in the company's fast-expanding factories on an industrial tract just outside Los Angeles.

Charney is an outlier. He is in his late thirties and running the single-largest maker of 100 percent U.S.-manufactured clothing. He makes T-shirts and other so-called commodities that are seen by American Apparel's largely young, urban customers as anything but basic. These are not the oversized Hanes and Fruit of the Loom T-shirts of the boomer generation.

In just a few years, American Apparel's store base has grown from a handful of LA locations to encompass far-flung neighborhoods of New York and San Francisco, Tokyo and Paris, Amsterdam and London. American Apparel sales topped $250 million in 2005, according to the company—a threefold increase over 2003 sales of about $80 million. Charney has done all of this while paying two or more times the minimum wage to the company's Los Angeles workers—a fact that has caused friction with apparel-industry unions representing workers.

Move in Different Circles

Finally, it is part of leadership to create a structure to support you and vet your big ideas. You are not likely to find such support from the small thinkers. You need people who inspire you. You must consult a diverse group of experts and move around in different circles in your professional and social life.

Socialize with people who are not part of your own work sphere on a regular basis. Go for exceptional people and mingle within an eclectic group. Artists, entrepreneurs, mountain climbers, video game designers, inventors. Invite them to a meeting or social event. Familiarize yourself with their work. Find out what makes them tick.

Many big thinkers have spent their lives cultivating eclectic interests and moving around in diverse circles. Take Wikipedia founder Jimmy Wales.

Wikipedia, the online, user-generated encyclopedia that has dwarfed the scope of any print resource in history, was pioneered by a visionary young man with extremely wide-ranging interests and pursuits. Wales started out studying finance in college to be an academic, but left his PhD program to go trade options in Chicago instead. After a few years, he took his savings and moved to San Diego to join the flock of start-ups. Wales's venture was an Internet portal with pornographic videos and blogs, among other things. He read avidly and widely. He was a fan of Enlightenment thinkers and was also inspired by Friedrich Hayek's 1945 free-market manifesto *The Use of Knowledge in Society*. The book's message—that anyone's knowledge is partial, and truth comes from people pooling their knowledge collectively—was a philosophical basis for the radical and contrarian idea of Wikipedia. Wales also immersed himself in learning about the open-source movement in software, inspired by *The Cathedral and the Bazaar*, written by the movement's founder, Eric Raymond.

Wales not only soaked up fresh ideas, he was also prone to experimenting, willing to make mistakes, and eager to learn from them. His first online encyclopedia, Nupedia, was a failure—it solicited scholars to write paid articles, just like a traditional encyclopedia. Only later did he try, on a lark, the idea of using "wiki" technology (which allows online editing open to everyone, not just programmers). Wales did not expect much from his experiment. But within a year, Wikipedia had twenty thousand entries, and he began to realize he was onto something big. It took a leader like Jimmy Wales, with the diverse interests and connections in philosophy, finance, and software design—and the willingness to try out a ridiculous gamble—to make it a reality.

Once Again, Should We Replace Executives with Robots?

The answer is a professorial "it depends."

If you think that management and leadership are all about analytics, number skills, and solving well-defined problems—by all means, replace your executives with robots. However, if you want executives to be innovative, think big, and lead others, then, sorry, you are still better off with people.

When you are selecting leaders for Big Think, I advise choosing those who show guts, passion, and perseverance, who have an agenda and move in different circles. They will be the leaders who build organizational structures and processes that last. They want Big Think to be not just one successful project. Their true interest will be much bigger—making Big Think sustainable.

-7-

Sustaining
Big Think

From Sisyphus to Odysseus

T HE CHALLENGE for Big Think leaders who engineer bold change is not just to set up one breakthrough strategy or initiative. It is not just launching the New Beetle car but revamping the Volkswagen brand as a whole. Not just creating W Hotels but rethinking a hotel conglomerate such as Starwood Hotels and Resorts Worldwide. Not just designing the RAZR but repositioning the whole of Motorola's electronic products. The challenge is formidable. You must weave Big Think into the fabric of the organization. The impact of one initiative must be expanded. The processes that led to it must continue to yield more bold initiatives. To do that, you must get the entire organization moving. You must promote permanent change.

Managing change—yuck, I hate that phrase—is difficult. It is difficult, as long as you think about it as managing change. The process must go much deeper, to the heart, to the soul of the individual and the organization. You must understand human motivation, the human condition. When people and organizations will not move, you may be dealing with powerful existential forces, not just organizational ones.

THE SQUARE MILE, LONDON

Josh Adams, a literature major–turned–MBA who has worked with me on several projects, is accompanying me at a strategy meeting of a major financial firm.

After several hours of discussion, we are getting nowhere. Even though they have decided to invest resources in bold strategic thinking, the executives across the table from us appear stymied by a lack of clear project ownership, a dour sense of the project's workload, and a cautious and conventional perspective of the options. Worst of all, they have just told us that part of the project must be declared out of scope, because it belongs to another department. I scribble three lines on a piece of paper and quietly slip it over to Josh.

Didi: Well, shall we go?

Gogo: Yes, let us go.

They do not move.

Josh smiles at me. We have done this exchange many times before. The lines of dialogue from the play *Waiting for Godot* are a signal for us to use one of our "existential interventions," as we call them, to get a group that is stuck moving.[1]

Theater of the Absurd

Playwright Samuel Beckett has subtitled *Waiting for Godot* a "tragicomedy in two acts." The play, and Beckett's work, has been characterized as "theater of the absurd." *Waiting for Godot* includes two main characters, Vladimir and Estragon (also called "Didi" and "Gogo"), who stand at a roadside to wait for someone referred to as "Godot." They engage in conversations until a boy arrives telling them that Godot will not arrive today but definitely tomorrow. Act 2, playing the next day, repeats the same story with minor variations.

The play has been interpreted as signifying the meaninglessness of human life. The characters are often compared to Sisyphus, the figure in Greek mythology who was condemned to endlessly repeat the same task of pushing a rock up a mountain,

Sisyphus pushing rock

only to see it roll down again.[2] Sounds like many corporate meetings to me. Beckett himself refused to provide any interpretation as to what his play is about and what it means. "It means what it says," he responded.[3]

Most people find Beckett's existentialist play quite depressing. Existentialism has become a kind of pop philosophy for gloomy, sardonic twenty-year-olds. But when I read Beckett as a high school and college student, I found the play amusing and, strangely enough, inspiring. In fact, the overall existentialist message—that life is a meaningless struggle until one finds one's own meaning—really gets my juices going. Rather than cause for despair, I see it as a call to action: "Let us take life into our own hands."

To get out of your corporate existential drift, I recommend you do the same. Think of it this way: "Corporate life is a meaningless struggle unless I provide it with my own meaning." Most likely, however, you will not find that much meaning in routine tasks and doing only what is expected. But you may find it if you truly think big about your work. Try becoming a "Big Thinky Head."

"Big Thinky Heads"

At some point, we were all creative and thinking big—unconstrained by convention, drawing wild associations, believing anything was possible. Back then, as young children, we had dreams. As teenagers, too, we still felt we could change the world, have an impact. Until we were told what can't be done, what we shouldn't do. Until we were told that life is struggle. Until we got our first job and started reading the existentialists.

The Museum of Modern Art in New York runs a family program sponsored by the Ford Motor Company, which I have attended with my seven-year-old son. It's refreshing to hear your children talk about works of the impressionists and post-impressionists, about Pollack and Picasso, as well as contemporary artists. Young children haven't yet read the art history books that tell them what the works mean. They are not skilled enough to read the text displays next to the work that tell them what to think about them. So, they make up their own, highly creative stories and interpretations about each work.

There are some adults, too, who get excited like children. They are experimenters and observers of the wonders of the world. They believe that anything is possible and want to make it happen.

So one afternoon, I asked my seven-year-old son what to call them. He replied instantly, "Big Thinky Heads." I thought, "Eureka!" I found the term original, playful, and yet quite descriptive of the idea I wanted to convey.

Big Problems Need Big Thinky Heads

Big problems need Big Thinky Heads because they maintain the childlike belief that any big problem can be solved. Consider global poverty, for a moment. Roughly half of the world's population is caught in a trap of poverty and reaping no benefits from globalization. Several Big Thinky Heads are determined to do something about it.

Bill and Melinda Gates are approaching the problem by thinking big about the impact of disease. If health problems, and AIDS in particular, are trapping people in a cycle of poverty, then perhaps the best investment for long-term economic development is in public health. The Bill & Melinda Gates Foundation has therefore invested heavily in vaccine distribution and disease prevention and treatment, and in 2006 it announced a $287 million donation to fund global research toward an AIDS vaccine.

Bangladeshi entrepreneur Muhammad Yunus is tackling world poverty from a different angle: from the bottom up. Yunus received the 2006 Nobel Peace Prize for his work championing the model of microcredit, running a for-profit business that loans money to women, the poor, even homeless beggars, to help them become financially self-sufficient. Sometimes the loans are for less than $50. Microcredit was a bold idea when Yunus started. At the time, none of the banks in Bangladesh wanted to take on the presumed risk of loaning money to poor people with zero assets to use as collateral. But Yunus discovered that the homeless beggars were more likely to repay their loans than the rich.

Jeffrey Sachs, my colleague at Columbia University, addresses poverty by looking at foreign aid.[4] Since the 1960s, poor countries have received more than $2.3 trillion dollars, but there has been no correlation between foreign aid and growth. Sachs's radical new approach to foreign aid is based on what he calls "clinical economics." Rather than requiring uniform policies for all developing countries, donors should consider geographical differences and conduct highly targeted interventions based on the needs of specific regions. Grants should be given instead of loans. Aid will focus on not just building infrastructure but maintaining it (versus the old think—building a clinic but refusing to pay to hire doctors).

In sum, Big Thinky heads bring a fresh and open mind to hard problems. What else do they do? What else are they like? Let us look at one of the biggest of all.

Einstein, Big Thinky head

Source: United Press International.

Einstein: Physics' Big Thinky Head

Albert Einstein is widely regarded as the epitome of genius and assumed by many to have been a serious, sober scientific guy. Actually, physics was fun for him, all about building models and mechanical devices. As a small boy, he was mesmerized by the invisible tug of magnetism on his father's compass.

At the age of sixteen, he was staring into a mirror curiously when he conceived of his first famous thought experiment. Wondering what would happen to his image if it were moving at the speed of light, the teenage experimenter concluded that the speed of light must be independent of its observer—a radical idea that years later became one of the two pillars of his theory of special relativity. Einstein's first published scientific paper came from examining the capillary forces in a drinking straw. This modest topic was his first stab at unifying the laws of physics, a grand goal he would continue for the rest of his life.

Like other Big Thinky Heads, Einstein did not do his best thinking by fitting into the establishment or bureaucracy. He dropped out of his first secondary school after clashing with authority, believing that creative thought was ill-served by the school's regimen of strict memorization. As a young man, he renounced his Swiss citizenship and became a man without a state. After college, he had irritated too many of his professors to get a teaching job, so he took a position in the patent office, where he was passed over for promotion. Working outside the circles of academia and the world's leading scientists, Einstein spent his free time developing his theories on his own. It was at the patent office that Einstein had his *annus mirabilis*, his "year of wonders," when he wrote four articles in short succession that upended the entire field of physics and established him as the greatest scientist of modern times.

Becoming a Big Thinky Head

Corporate Big Thinky Heads, the little Einsteins in organizations, share a lot in common with Einstein. For them, thinking is fun. Often, they are iconoclasts. Like Einstein, many corporate Big Thinky Heads can also have an eccentric maverick streak to them. Think Steve Jobs, Richard Branson, Larry Ellison.

If you are going to pursue Big Think, you must become a Big Thinky head yourself—with fresh perspectives, a sense of possibility, and a little bit of wackiness.

As a leader, if you want to create a culture that sustains Big Think, you must do more than this. You must hire Big Thinky

Heads and inspire them by providing an environment of organized stimulation.

Organized Stimulation

By *organized stimulation*, I am referring to a deliberate and planned process that exposes employees constantly to exciting new information and new environments that are relevant to the project at hand and that stimulate thought. Organized stimulation that triggers mental connections is key for creativity. It is the brain food for Big Thinky Heads.

Not long ago, Samsung's reputation was as a B2B manufacturer (memory chips) with low-grade consumer products (cheap household appliances). When Samsung chairman Kun-Hee Lee set out to reposition the company as a cutting-edge designer of high-quality electronics, he knew the culture of the company had to change. His plan was to create what is now known as the Innovative Design Lab of Samsung (IDS) to give designers and other staffers exposure to the principles of design from around the world.

Samsung recruited leaders from the Art Center College of Design in Pasadena, California, to give designers and, later, marketing and engineering employees a global perspective on how Korean design fits in with the rest of the world.[5] For part of its program, IDS leaders brought the Samsung employees to cultural centers like New York, Florence, Athens, and Beijing to personally experience lifestyles and culture. The purpose was to help them understand consumer behavior around the world and learn what was truly unique about Korean design. The impact that IDS has contributed to the value of the Samsung brand is reflected in hundreds of new products that have won high-profile design awards and worldwide praise.

In my own work with companies, I frequently use organized stimulation as an intervention technique. When we get stuck on an issue in the classroom or boardroom, we head out—for a walking tour or off to a museum. For example, I have taken executives to museums and sculpture gardens to get them to think out of the box by relating contemporary art objects to their business issues. Putting people in a new context can speed up the incubation phase of creativity and increase the chance of an "aha!" experience. I myself have had some of my best ideas outside my office—for example, in museums, during opera performances, while sitting in a football stadium, or when getting a haircut.

Work/Play Balance

So, let us say you have hired some Big Thinky Heads and provided an environment of organized stimulation for them. How do you make them most productive? It turns out that for Big Thinky heads, productivity is not all about work. It is also about play, and the right balance between the two.

People working at a Big Think organization need *work/play balance*—the right mix of work and playful activities: work that is play, and play that produces work results.

What I call work/play balance is not to be confused with *work/life balance*. Today, employees and employers are very concerned about work/life balance—that is, the right mix of work time and free time (or family time). For employees, it is about lifestyle: how to take care of family and other private needs as working hours are getting longer and expectations at work higher. For employers, it is about productivity—how to increase people's ability to participate in the workforce and be productive while taking care of family and personal needs. Firms have established various policies that are supposed to foster a better work/life balance and avoid the stress resulting from a mismatch of work and life. These policies run the gamut from parental leaves and flexible work hours to offering exercise and yoga. Even my seven-year-old participates in wellness sessions as part of the second-grade curriculum at his school.

I am all for work/life balance. But, for me, the real balance is not about work versus other aspects of life. It is about balance *at work*.

Big Think assignments and projects require certain work styles. Big Think work is not repetitive work. It is not a day of unproductive meetings. It is not about showing up, doing your job, and leaving the office at five o'clock (or at seven or nine). Big Think is stimulating, creative work. Big Think flourishes in a work/play environment.

At the "Googleplex," Google's headquarters in Mountain View, California, work spaces have been designed for a work/play environment. Bicycles and large rubber exercise balls are found on many floors; press clippings from around the world are posted on bulletin boards everywhere. Googlers often just hang out to discuss arcane IP addressing issues. Engineers have "20 percent time" in which they're free to pursue projects that they are passionate about. This freedom has produced Google News, Google Suggest, AdSense for Content, and Orkut—products that might otherwise have taken an entire start-up to launch.

Is 20 percent play the right amount? I think so. Make it 10 to 30, depending on the organization (government or ad agency) and the type of work (account executive versus copy writer), but 50 percent is definitely too much. Play must happen within the context of work, not the other way around. Play must be used as a stimulant, not as a purpose of its own. Work must be play.

That is why out-of-context creativity or team-building exercises, which are just focused on play—such as asking two people to draw a face by contributing elements one after the other, or jumping together in a group on a trampoline—do not work. Sure they are fun; sure they make for an engaging conversation; however, they are too far removed from business practice. I am also a bit critical of the Ping-Pong and foosball tables and Philippe Starck chairs I have seen in ad agencies. Sure, Ping-Pong and foosball help you unwind; sure, these chairs are cool. But do they promote creativity and Big Think? Businesses should not pay employees for just having fun but for work/play balance that produces results. And one of the best ways to get employees to produce results is to give them a stake in the business.

Entreprenurial Spirit

If you are a leader in a medium-size or large organization and you are serious about sustaining Big Think, you need to do more than hire Big Thinky Heads and provide them with organizational stimulation and work/play balance. You must instill an entrepreneurial spirit among the managers who work with you. The term *entrepreneurial spirit* (or *Unternehmergeist*) was coined by Austrian economist Joseph Schumpeter (1883–1950), who fifty years after his death became a sort of hipster icon during the dot-com days.[6] Schumpeter believed that individuals with an entrepreneurial spirit produce innovation and growth for the economy. Entrepreneurship continues to be associated with risk taking and grasping opportunities.

How Can You Instill an Entrepreneurial Spirit?

Entrepreneurship will flourish in an organization that is run not as a monolithic, slow bureaucracy but as a dynamic culture of organizational units that manage projects speedily and at their own risk. At the core of these organizational units are risk-taking individuals with a strong urge to identify and capture opportunities that build future value for customers and the firm.

Managers must fully own projects. They must be fully in charge. They plan the project; they select team members; they are responsible for outcomes. Team leaders are fully empowered to make decisions. They are thus given autonomy in managing projects. After receiving broad-based guidelines about goals and objectives, they are on their own and free to take the project in the direction that they prefer.

Whole Foods' Entrepreneurship

One of the most striking examples of an entrepreneurial culture is Whole Foods. The organizational structure of Whole Foods is a radical experiment in democratic capitalism that has been informed by CEO John Mackey's readings of Japanese management books from the 1970s. The focus throughout the organization is on staff empowerment, autonomy, and teamwork.

Local stores are given a great deal of autonomy and responsibility. Regional managers are allowed to design each new store. In-store teams decide what foods to stock. When I visited its flagship store in Austin, Texas, its home base, I noticed lots of different kinds of produce that I have not seen stocked at the New York City stores.

But the real focus of entrepreneurship is the smaller unit of the "staff teams" within each store—the produce team, the bakery team, the checkout team, and so on. Each team gets to vote on whether new hires become permanent after thirty days—and it requires a two-thirds vote to keep them on. Team members have a powerful incentive to insist that their new compatriots are the best because everyone gets pay bonuses based on the team's productivity results, assessed every four weeks. The result is that team members are pushed to perform by their peers, not by the managers above them.

The company uses transparency to build trust and foster healthy internal competition. As part of its "no secrets" management, all salaries are listed in a book any employee can see. A flood of other data on productivity and profitability is available to all employees so they can see how they are competing against each other for their bonuses. The company shares so much information that the Securities and Exchange Commission has classified every Whole Foods employee as an "insider" with regard to stock trading.

Employees are constantly pushing and learning from each other. There is a lot of lateral learning—finding out what colleagues are doing successfully and spreading the practice within the organization. Peer review is done in the form of store tours and a customer snapshot that allows each store to get feedback and evaluation from others. All of this learning helps staff improve, as teams compete against teams, stores against stores, and regions against regions—for bonuses, recognition, and promotions.

Sound cutthroat? Whole Foods tries hard to make its workers happy, too. With the productivity they are able to yield, the company can afford to cover 100 percent of health-care premiums for all full-time workers, pay workers a living wage, and make stock options broadly available. Top executive salaries are capped at fourteen times the average pay. Dress code is liberal. And all full-timers are paid to do twenty hours of volunteer work each year. It is no surprise that Whole Foods has ranked in *Fortune*'s "100 Best Companies to Work For" list for nine years. But even Whole Foods knows that entrepreneurial spirit is not just a matter of the right balance of incentives and competition. Whenever the company opens a new store, it tries to tap employees from existing stores for 30 percent of the new positions. Whole Foods says it must spread the culture—like a yogurt culture spreading to a new vat of milk.

Organizational Silos: The Ultimate Evil

You can hire Big Thinky Heads, offer them the right environment and work/play balance, instill an entrepreneurial spirit, and you may still fail. All the right people, environments, and attitudes are nothing unless you address organizational silos. They are the ultimate corporate evil (excuse the term *evil*: I was born Catholic and am writing this book during the latter days of the presidency of George W. Bush). To achieve and sustain Big Think, you must exorcise this evil from your organization.

In most organizations, employees are relatively isolated, operating only within their own defined function or department (sales, marketing, manufacturing, etc.). Moreover, within that function or department, there is a strict hierarchy: actions are performed and supervised in a military-style top-down manner. As a result, there is little communication between departments. Project teams are often staffed with members of one department only and perhaps one outsider who rarely shows up at the meetings, and the rest of the team likes it that way. There is a lot of resistance to anything "not invented here." These structures and behaviors prevent Big Think in many organizations.

One company in which the silo mentality has nearly spelled tragedy is Sony. For fifty years, Sony was a market leader in many categories. Sony produced outstanding products, and one innovation after another. In 1950, Sony, originally the producer of an electronic rice cooker, introduced the first magnetic tape recorder. Then followed the first transistor radio, the first all-transistor TV set, the first color videocassette recorder. In 1979 Sony launched the Walkman. And soon after, the Trinitron television set.

But at the coming of the digital age, Sony products had one fundamental flaw: they did not communicate with each other, or only in an extremely cumbersome way. A case in point is the Network Walkman, a digital music player that Sony launched more than two years before the iPod. Getting the music into the device was absurdly difficult. Within five years, from 2001 to 2006, the stock dropped 45 percent.

The reason for the poor communication between products can be found in the company's silo organization. Product engineers worked independently of software designers. Each product was supported by a different marketing team. The company—which should have been capitalizing on the digital revolution because it had great electronics products, great audio content (through Sony Music), and great video content (through Sony Pictures), all under one roof—failed miserably in exploiting the convergence among its business units.

I witnessed this sad state of affairs when I consulted for Sony Electronics in the United States at the dawn of the digital era. Sony was organized around product groups, not customer segments. Product managers used small ad agencies, and each agency was in charge of just a few products. I recommended that Sony adopt a more integrated approach to enhance the cross-selling of its products.

Yet Sony's problems continue today. Sony has the right technologies in all corners. Sir Howard Stringer, Sony's chairman and chief executive as of June 2005, has the right vision when he talks about entertaining the future and convergence, just as prior CEO Nobuyuki Idei did when he talked about "digital dream kids" and "dreaming with Sony." But the devil is in the details—here, the organizational structure—where innovation still happens in silos, whereas Big Think demands convergence and integration.

To make Big Think happen in your organization and to turn it into a sustainable force, you must break down these silos. There will still be some hierarchy. There will still be functions and departments—accounting, marketing, legal, and so on. But multiple perspectives must exist, be respected, and be developed through collaborative work. Employees will not wear functional hats; they will have an interdisciplinary mind-set.

Interdisciplinary Mind-set

The term *interdisciplinary* is often used in the context of academic collaborations when researchers and specialists from different fields work together to solve a problem. They share the conviction that drawing boundaries around fields prevents progress on really important issues. To address the holy grails and big issues in science or the arts—such as the origin of the universe, pandemics, global warming, the structure of the mind, or the identity of humans in modern society—an interdisciplinary mind-set is needed.

Interdisciplinary innovation, in the form of interdisciplinary design in industrial production, technology conversion, and nanotechnology, is also seen as the new trend in engineering. Similarly, Big Think in business requires interdisciplinary thinking. In business, as in academia, big issues require people to go beyond what they are most familiar with. They must stretch their imaginations to connect even quite distinct fields. For example, engineers must become customer driven and appreciate customer input early on in the development process. Customer advocates must learn to appreciate the perspective of engineers and other experts who know best what is feasible and what are the latest applications of new technology. Similarly, designers of the retail experience must understand how it connects with online selling, and vice versa.

Developing and implementing Big Think strategies on an ongoing basis requires knowledge of different disciplines. Team members must assume different perspectives to generate and implement a Big Think strategy. They must work together on hard problems.

Interdisciplinary thinking is about active learning from each other, cross-fertilization of ideas, as well as coordinated and integrated action plans for implementation. To make it happen, traditional job functions must give way to new job descriptions that embrace an interdisciplinary mind-set. Finally, incentive systems, measurements, and rewards should be based, in part, on interdisciplinary work. Assess, for example, what percentage of your new products are coming from interdisciplinary work, compared with purely disciplinary innovation.

Conclusion

We have reached the outermost circle of the Big Think strategy framework—sustaining bold thinking and decision making within the organization. As figure 7-3 shows, the inner-circle tasks of Big Think are the management of a Big Think project—by sourcing ideas, evaluating them, turning them into a strategy, and executing the strategy. Throughout Big Think project management, you must leverage bold ideas and constantly fight small thinking. Leading a Big Think project requires guts, passion, and perseverance; you must have an agenda and consult various people by moving in different circles.

Making Big Think sustainable is the hardest task of all. To succeed, you need the right people, environments, and organizational structure. You must start with the right people, Big Thinky heads, who get excited about new ideas with a childlike fervor. For Big Think to flourish, these people must be empowered by the organization and stimulated by the environment around them. Giving employees the opportunity to own projects, make key decisions, and ultimately be held accountable

FIGURE 7-1

Big Think strategy framework

for their successes and failures can build an entrepreneurial spirit that not only sustains Big Think but spreads it throughout other parts of the organization. Finally, Big Think cannot be sustained in an environment filled with organizational silos, but can become infectious among people with an interdisciplinary mind-set.

What is the alternative? Remember Sisyphus, pushing his rock forever up the mountain? For the existentialist philosopher Albert Camus, Sisyphus was the symbol of the human condition—and of futile office work in the modern organization. (Think of the cartoon character Dilbert.) "The workman of today works every day in his life at the same tasks, and this fate is no less absurd," wrote Camus.[7]

Indeed, Small Think is despair—and we should leave it behind. Big Think, on the other hand, can salvage us from the daily pains of our habitual existence, by letting us create our own bold vision for our lives and work and transforming each of us from Sisyphus to Odysseus.

Epilogue

THIS BRINGS US to the end of the book—and my journey. I trust that you have been inspired by Odysseus, Mahler, and *Fitzcarraldo*...

DESCENDING FROM 30,000 FEET ON A BOEING 747

I am torn from my sleep. "Where am I? *Wo ist das Pferd?* Where am I going? What time zone am I in?"

"*Hello, this is your captain speaking!*" blares the voice in my headset. "*We are now on our final approach. Please put your seats in the full upright position and fasten your seat belts. All electronic devices should now be turned off for the remainder of the flight. It was a pleasure serving you and we hope to see you again soon.*"

I cannot believe I slept the entire flight. What a waste. I wanted to get started writing my book, finally. And here I have wasted eleven precious hours. I will never get anywhere with this Big Think concept.

But suddenly I have an idea for a beginning. Why not start the book as if it were a novel? I pull out my laptop and quickly start to type.

"*Geneva, Switzerland.* I am in the front seat of the taxi. In the backseat: two partners of a certain world-famous consulting firm that advises clients on strategy. We are heading to the airport after several days of intense work on one of their projects. 'We really have a tough time thinking big,' the conversation starts."

A flight attendant materializes. "Sir, please, you must turn off your laptop. We will be landing at any moment."

Post Roll

All the characters and companies
featured in this book are real.
All scene locations were visited by the author
during the writing of this book,
although some locations have been shifted
to honor nondisclosure agreements
and to ease corporate apprehension.

Marty Homlish went on to add $1 billion
in brand value at SAP in one year.

Silvia Lagnado of Dove was promoted to
group vice president of Unilever Foods.

Nick Peterson returned home to Minnesota.

Sisyphus is still pushing his rock.

The author followed his calling and
did build a Trojan horse in Shanghai.
Information about the project
is available on
http://www.meetschmitt.com/trojanhorse.

The *Schmitt Shanghai Trojan Horse*
stands today as a monument
to big thinkers everywhere.

Photo by Jiang Ling

Notes

Chapter 1

1. Key books and articles on strategy include: Michael Porter, *Competitive Strategy* (New York: Free Press, 1980); Gary Hamel and C. K. Prahalad, "The Core Competence of the Corporation," *Harvard Business Review*, Vol. 68, no. 3, May–June 1990: 79–93; Geoffrey Moore, *Inside the Tornado: Strategies for Developing, Leveraging, and Surviving Hypergrowth Markets* (New York: HarperBusiness, 1995; Henry Mintzberg, *The Rise and Fall of Strategic Planning* (New York: The Free Press, 1994).

Chapter 2

1. This model of creativity goes back to Graham Wallace, who first presented it in his work *Art of Thought* in 1926. The first and last phases are commonly referred to as "convergent thinking"; the second and third phases are referred to as divergent thinking (see Joy Paul Guilford, "Creativity," *American Psychologist* 15 (1950): 444–454.

2. Kenneth M. Heilman, *Creativity and the Brain* (New York: Psychology Press, 2005).

3. Bernd Schmitt, *Customer Experience Management* (New York: Wiley, 2003).

4. Eric von Hippel, *Democratizing Innovation* (Cambridge, MA: The MIT Press, 2006).

Chapter 3

1. James Surowiecki, *The Wisdom of Crowds: Why the Many Are Smarter Than the Few and How Collective Wisdom Shapes Business, Economies, Societies and Nations* (New York: Random House, 2004).

2. Olivier Toubia, "Idea Generation, Creativity, and Incentives," *Marketing Science* 25, no. 5 (2006): 411–425.

3. H. G. Wells, *World Brain* (London: Meuthuen, 1938).

4. Malcolm Gladwell, *Blink: The Power of Thinking Without Thinking* (Boston: Back Bay Books, 2005).

5. CNN.com, "Readers Brainstorm on Future of New Orleans," posted on cnn.com on October 5, 2005.

6. Podcast interview with Deepak Advani conducted as part of the 2007 Conference on Innovative Marketing, which I co-organized at Columbia Business School in New York City in fall 2006.

Chapter 4

1. The most authoritative book on the topic of Japanese beef production remains the classic by John Longworth, *Beef in Japan: Production, Marketing and Trade* (St. Lucia: University of Queensland Press, 1983).

2. The four Big Think strategy quadrants are derived, in part, by combining key aspects of the prior strategy literature. Critical insights on organizational capabilities can be found in research on the resource-based view of the firm including John Fahy and Alan Smithee, "Strategic Management and the Resource Based View of the Firm," *Academy of Marketing Science Review* 10 (1999); Birger Wernerfelt, "A Resource-Based View of the Firm," *Strategic Management Journal* 5 (1984): 171–180; and Edith Penrose, *The Theory of Growth of the Firm* (Oxford: Blackwell, 1959). For research on customer value see

Shelby D. Hunt and Robert M. Morgan, "The Comparative Advantage Theory of Competition," *Journal of Marketing* 59 (1995): 1–15. My ideas of a business network quadrant and of a market ecosystem quadrant have been influenced by the notion of an innovation ecosystem presented by Ron Adner, "Match Your Innovation Strategy to Your Innovation Ecosystem," *Harvard Business Review*, April 2006, 98–107.

3. Michael E. Porter, *Competitive Strategy* (New York: Free Press, 1980).

4. Michael Treacy and Fred Wiersema, *The Discipline of Market Leaders: Choose Your Customers, Narrow Your Focus, Dominate Your Market* (New York: Perseus Books Group, 2005).

5. Leonard Bernstein, "Mahler—His Time Has Come," *High Fidelity*, April 1967.

6. "Mahler's dirty fingers were all over the score," said a librarian (name withheld upon request) of the New York Public Library for the Performing Arts to my assistant on the phone.

7. Edward Reilly, "An Inventory of Musical Scores," *News About Mahler Research* 2 (1977).

8. Larry Bossidy and Ram Charan, *Execution: The Discipline of Getting Things Done* (New York: Crown Business, 2002).

Chapter 5

1. Sun Tzu, *The Art of War*, trans. William Lidwell.

2. Roger Ebert, "Fitzcarraldo," originally written in January 1982; available on rogerebert.com.

3. Ibid.

4. Ibid.

5. Publicity data is reported in *Red* 6, no. 8 (published by Ogilvy and Mather).

Chapter 6

1. Joseph Weizenbaum, *Computer Power and Human Reason*, (New York: W. H. Freeman, 1976).

2. Alan Turing, "Computing Machinery and Intelligence," *Mind* 59, no. 236 (1950): 433–460.

3. Robert House and Philip M. Podsakoff, "Leadership Effectiveness: Past Perspectives and Future Directions for Research" in *Organizational Behavior: The State of the Science*, ed. Jerald Greenberg (Hillsdale, NJ: Erlbaum, 1994).

4. Bernd Schmitt and David Rogers, "SAP: Building a Leading Technology Brand," Case study, Columbia Business School, 2006.

5. Solomon Asch, "Opinions and Social Pressure," *Scientific American*, November 1955, 31–35.

6. Stanley Milgram, "Behavioral Study of Obedience," *Journal of Abnormal and Social Psychology* 67 (1963): 371–378.

7. Serge Moscovici and C. Nemeth, "Social Influence II: Minority Influence," in *Social Psychology: Classic and Contemporary Integrations*, ed. C. Nemeth (Chicago: Rand McNally, 1974).

8. Carlos Ghosn, *Shift: Inside Nissan's Historic Survival* (New York: Random House, 2006).

9. Quote from project Web site: www.laptop.org and wiki.laptop.org

10. David Kirkpatrick, "I'd Like to Teach the World to Type," *Fortune*, November 16, 2005.

Chapter 7

1. Samuel Beckett, *Waiting for Godot* (New York: Grove Press, 1954).

2. Albert Camus, *The Myth of Sisyphus* (New York: Vintage International, reissued edition 1991; originally published in 1942 in French as *Le Mythe de Sisyphe*).

3. Jonathan Croall, *The Coming of Godot: A Short History of a Masterpiece* (London: Oberon Books, 2006) 91.

4. Jeffrey Sachs, *The End of Poverty* (New York: Penguin, 2005).

5. "Samsung's Lessons in Design," *The Journal of Business and Design* 9, no. 1.

6. T. K. McGraw, "Schumpeter Ascending: Re-emerging Intellectual Interest in Entrepreneurship, Innovation, and Economic Development," *American Scholar* 60 (summer 1991): 371–392.

7. Camus, *The Myth of Sisyphus*.

Index

Abercrombie & Fitch (A&F),
    51–52
Absolut vodka, 112
ADK, 84–86
Advanced Micro Devices
    (AMD), 134
Advani, Deepak, 77
advertising and bold
    communications, 116
Agamemnon, 15, 127
Amazon.com, 94
American Apparel, 136
American Express, 36
AmorePacific Corporation, 41,
    45
analysis plus instinct, 65–69
Apple Inc., 7, 73, 98, 134
artificial intelligence, 121, 125
assumptions
    challenging, 8, 10, 42–43, 95
    developing alternatives to, 45
    testing and reaffirming, 45
attention getters, finding,
    114–115

Audi, 116
avatar, 12

bananapapaya.com, 57
Barbiere di Siviglia, 11
Beckett, Samuel, 141–142
benchmarking, outside-
    industry, 34–40
Bernstein, Leonard, 99
big ideas
    business impact, 72–73
    communications impact,
        73–75
    creativity, 70–72
    defendability of, 77–78
    feasibility of, 76–77
    getting from customers, 54–55
    internal fit of, 78–79
big splash in market
    bold communications,
        116–118
    finding attention getters,
        114–115

Big Think, 2
    achieving growth in changing
        environment, 5
    altering nature of competition,
        6
    business success and, 6–8
    leadership, 5, 8, 22–23
    versus Small Think, 3–6
    strategy quadrants, 22
    strategy tasks, 20–23
Big Think strategy quadrants,
    87–88
Big Think strategy types, 92–99
Big Think teams 57, 113
Big Thinky Heads
    Albert Einstein, 145–146
    becoming, 146–147
    big problems needing,
        143–144
    hiring, 147
    interdisciplinary mind-set,
        155–157
    organized stimulation,
        147–148
    work/play balance, 148–150
Bill & Melinda Gates
    Foundation, 144
Boateng, Ozwald, 66
bold communications
    help from customers, 118–119
    maximum impact, 116–117
bold ideas, 14–15
BP's "Helios House," 48–49
brain, role in creativity, 27–31
brands and trends, 31–34
Branson, Richard, 44, 95, 146
budgets, 104
Burger King, 74
Burj Al Arab hotel, 114

businesses
    environment and strategies, 13
    impact of big ideas, 72–73
    resources and competence, 13
    success and Big Think, 6–8
    Trojan horse and, 2
business networks, 22, 87–88,
    89
buy-in, 109–110

Camus, Albert, 158
capturing strategy concept
    84–87
Chanel, Coco, 47
Charles, Ray, 81
Charney, Dov, 136
classic strategy model, 13–15
clustering ideas, 59–62
    analytical evaluation criteria,
        62
    evaluating each idea, 61
    involving right people, 62
    music at Starbucks, 60–62
CNN.com Web site and
    reinventing New Orleans,
    75–76
combining the (seemingly)
    incompatible, 30, 31–34
commonsense knowledge and
    creativity, 126
communications
    impact of big ideas, 73–75
    old and new models of, 86
competition, 89
    altering nature of, 6
    defendable ideas, 77–78
    inspiration from, 35–36
corporate mission, 50

costs, 104
craigslist.org, 118–119
creative experience model, 39
creativity
  big ideas, 70–72
  brain's role in, 27–31
  challenging conventional
    wisdom, 16
  dreams and, 29–30
  phases of the creative process,
    27–28
customers
  coproducing product, 57–58
  getting big ideas from, 54–55
  helping with bold
    communications, 118–119
  idea-sourcing process, 21
  innovation from, 52–57
  lead users, 55–56
  tapping for creative idea
    sourcing, 55–56
customer value, 17, 88, 89–90

David, Dharshini, 135
defendability, 77–78
Dell, Michael, 43
Dell Computers, 8, 13, 39–40,
  88–89
Design Within Reach, 34–35
detergents, 42, 44
Die Meistersinger von
  Nürnberg, 62
digital music distribution, 7
do-it-yourself concept, 93–94
Dove, 9–10
  Campaign for Real Beauty, 10,
    116–118, 162
  Self-Esteem Fund, 10

dreams and creativity, 29–30
Dubai economic development
  program, 114–115
Dylan, Bob, 81

Ebert, Roger, 107, 109
Einstein, Albert, 145–146
Ellison, Larry, 146
employees motivating
  themselves, 110
entrepreneurial spirit, 150–153
essence strategy, 94–97
evaluating ideas, 21
  clustering ideas, 59–62
  expert decision making, 62–64
  independently and
    anonymously, 63–64
  instinct plus analysis, 66–69
  Meistersinger syndrome, 62–64
  reinventing New Orleans,
    75–76
executing Big Think strategies,
    103–104
  big splash in marketplace, 107
  milestones and plan for quick
    wins, 106
  overcoming inertia and
    resistance, 106
  rolling out successfully over
    time, 106
  tapping into employees'
    dreams, 109–110
existentialism, 142, 158
experience
  Aha! Experience, 28, 148
  Audi driving experience, 116
  commoditization of Starbucks
    experience, 135

experience (*continued*)
creative experience model, 39
experiential values, 89
retail experience, 156

fashion styles, 47
feasibility, 76–77
FedEx, 43
FIFA World Cup, 119
finding attention getters, 114–115
Fitzcarraldo, 107–109
Flavin, Dan, 68
Forbes, Robert, 34
Ford Motor Company, 143

game theory, 78
Gates, Bill, 134, 143–144
Gates, Melinda, 143–144
Geek Squad, 39–40
Gelb, Peter, 10–11
General Electric, 17–19
Gerstner, Lou, 8
Ghosn, Carlos, 131
Givenchy, 66
global poverty, 143–144
Google
AdSense for Content, 149
Google News, 149
Google Suggest, 149
One Laptop Per Child
(OLPC) and, 134
Orkut, 149
systematic unfolding of
strategy score, 102
"Googleplex," 149
gourmet products, 8
Grameen Bank, 95

growth, achieving in changing
environment, 5
Gucci, 47, 94
Gucci Group, 35
Gupta, Sunil, 39
guts
challenging long-held beliefs,
129–130
leadership and, 128–131
overcoming fears, 131
sticking with views against
pressure, 130

Han, Jin, 66
hard competencies, 88–89
Hayek, Friedrich, 137
Heilman, Kenneth, 28–29, 30
Henkel, 45
Herzog, Werner, 107–109
Hewlett-Packard, 8
H&M, 52
home furnishings market, 34
Homlish, Marty, 129–130, 162
House, Robert, 128
humans, differences from
robots, 126–127

IBM, 8, 14
idea clusters, 59–62, 71–72
ideas
creativity, 70–72
evaluation criteria, 70–74,
76–79
five idea sourcing tools, 30–31
structure to support, 136–138
turning into Big Think
strategy, 22, 83–104

idea-sourcing tools
  combining the (seemingly)
    incompatible, 30, 31–34
  innovation from customers,
    52–57
  killing sacred cows, 30–31,
    40–45
  outside-industry
    benchmarking, 30, 34–40
  stepping out of time frame, 31,
    46–49
  strategy stripping, 31, 49–52
Idei, Nobuyuki, 155
IKEA and do-it-yourself
  concept, 94
illumination, 27
Immelt, Jeffrey, 17–19
incubation, 27–28
industries
  creatively mapping insights
    and ideas to, 38–39
  identifying exemplary, 37–38
  looking for ideas outside,
    16–17
innovation from customers,
  52–57
instinct plus analysis, 66–69
integration strategy, 94
  combining incompatible ideas
    with business practices,
    95
  risks, 96–97
interdisciplinary mind-set,
  155–157
internal fit of big ideas, 78–79
Internet, 57
iPhone, 73
iPod, 7, 17, 98
iTunes, 7, 98

Jagger, Mick, 108
Jansons, Mariss, 99
JetBlue, 78
Jobs, Steve, 7, 134, 146
Jones, Norah, 81
Joyce Boutique Holdings, 40

Kekulé, Friedrich August, 30
Kellogg, John Harvey, 58
Kellogg, Will Keith, 58
Kellogg's Corn Flakes, 58
  spirituality and, 31, 33
killing sacred cows, 40–45
  adding new ingredients, 41
  change, 40–41
  mobile dry-clean detergent, 42
  wild and crazy ideas, 43
King, Stephen, 30
Kinski, Klaus, 108–109
Klein, Russ, 74
The Knot.com, 71–72

Lagnado, Silvia, 9–10, 162
Lavoie, Jim, 63–64
Lazarus, Shelly, 118
leadership, 8
  agendas, 135–136
  behaviors, 128–134
  Big Think, 22–23
  challenging long-held beliefs,
    129–130
  guts and, 128–131
  moving in different circles,
    136–138
  passion, 131–133
  perseverance, 133–134
  sticking to standards, 130–131

leadership (*continued*)
  structure to support ideas,
    136–138
Lee, Hae-Sun, 41
Lee, Kun-Hee, 19
Lenovo International, 77
Linden Lab, 12
LinkedIn, 11
Liu, David, 71
Liz Claiborne, 110
L.L.Bean, 52
long-held beliefs, challenging,
  129–130
Lotte Group, 103
Lucky Brand, 110
LVMH, 35

Ma, Adrienne, 40
Mackey, John, 8, 151
Madama Butterfly, 11
Mahler, Gustav, 99–103
managing change, 140
market ecosystem, 22, 90
markets, big splash in, 113–119
McCartney, Paul, 30
media and bold communica-
  tions, 116
Meistersinger Syndrome, 62–64,
  66
Merck, 35
Metropolitan Opera, 10–11, 14
microcredit, 144
milestones, 111–112
MINI car, 89, 93
minimalism, 47
minority influence, 130
MIT Media Lab, 133
Modo & Modo, 46–47

Moleskine notebook, 46–47
moving in different circles,
  136–138
multiple sclerosis (MS)
  medication, 90–93
Murdoch, Rupert, 134
Museum of Modern Art, 143
music
  at Starbucks, 60–62
  transforming industry, 7
MySpace, 11, 17, 90

Naganuma, Koichiro, 85–87
National Basketball Association
  (NBA), 132–133
Neeleman, David, 78
Negroponte, Nicholas, 133–134
new ideas, sourcing, 21
Newmark, Craig, 119
Nicklaus, Jack, 30
Nissan, 131
Nortel, 134
Nupedia, 138

Odysseus, 105–106, 127–128
The Odyssey (Homer), 127
Ogilvy & Mather, 117
Oh, D. J., 19–20
One Laptop Per Child (OLPC),
  133–134
online social networking, 11–13
opposition strategy, 93–94
  outside-industry
    benchmarking, 96
  questioning long-held
    assumptions, 95
  risks, 96–97

Oprah Winfrey Show, 118
organic food, 8
organizational capabilities, 22,
    87, 88–89
organizational silos, 4, 153–155
organizations
  Big Ideas and, 2, 78–79
  leadership, 22–23
  refusing to change, 42–43
  sustaining Big Think, 23
organized stimulation, 147–148
out-of-the-box thinking, 16
outside-industry
    benchmarking, 30, 34–40
  benchmarking team, 37
  conceptual model of problem
    area, 36–37
  identifying exemplary
    industries and companies,
    37–38
  identifying problem area, 36–37

Palm, 73
Palm Dubai, 114
Palmisano, Sam, 8
passion, 131–133
permanent change, 139–140
perseverance, 133–134
person-centered psychotherapy,
    122
Pfizer, 35
Pinakothek der Moderne, 68
planning for milestones and
    quick wins, 111–112
PlayStation, 129
Podsakoff, Philip, 128
Porter, Michael, 13, 92
Prada, 47, 94

productivity, 149
products
  adding new ingredients, 41
  change, 40–41
  customers coproducing, 57–58
  retro, 46–47
project manager, 109–110
pulling ship over the mountain,
    105–109

quick wins, 111–112

Ramnani, Vinita, 49
Raymond, Eric, 137
RealNetworks, 12
Reilly, Edward, 99
reinventing New Orleans,
    75–76
Research In Motion (RIM), 73
retro products, 46–47
Rite-Solutions, 63–64
Rite-View, 64
Ritz-Carlton hotel chain, 39
Robards, Jason, 108
robots
  differences from humans,
    126–127
  replacing executives, 138
Rogers, Carl, 122
Rogers, David, 101–102
Rolling Stones, 81
Roney, Carley, 71
Rosedale, Philip, 11–12

Sachs, Jeffrey, 144
sacred cows, 25–27

sacred cows (*continued*)
  detergent business, 44
  killing, 30–31, 40–45
Samsung, 19–20, 147–148
SAP, 129–130, 162
Schmidt und Kaiser, 119
Schultz, Howard, 135
Schumpeter, Joseph, 151
Second Life, 12–13, 90
service excellence model, 39
Singapore, 66–67, 115
Singapore Airlines, 39
Sisyphus, 141–142, 158, 163
Six Sigma, 18
Small Think
  versus Big Think, 3–6
  diluting core idea, 22
  ease of doing, 4–5
  hostage to quarterly earnings
    report, 4
  killing creativity, 4
  known territory, 4
  organization siloes, 4, 23
  standard procedures, 5
  sticking with status quo, 4
  stifling innovation, 4
Smith, Fred, 43
Smith & Hawken, 34
social networking online, 11–13
soft competencies, 88–89
Sony, 129, 154–155
sourcing ideas, 21, 27
standards, sticking to, 130–131
Starbucks, 135
  CD-burning kiosks, 81
  music at, 60–62, 72
  outcomes of music initiative,
    81–82

steaks and strategy, 25–27
stepping out of time frame, 31,
    46–49
Stern, David, 132–133
strategic planning
  alternative approach to, 16–17
  creative processes and, 6
  Small Think and, 16, 21
  value of, 16
strategies
  big splash in market, 113–119
  capturing concept, 84–87
  classic model, 13
  customer value created by,
    22
  development and execution,
    2
  essence strategy, 94–95
  executing, 103–104
  integration strategy, 94
  opposition strategy, 93–94
  tasks for Big Think, 20–23
  transcendence strategy, 95
  turning ideas into, 83–104
  types, 92–99
strategy quadrants, 87–92
strategy stripping, 31, 49–52
Stringer, Howard, 155
Sun Tzu, 105
supermarket industry, 7–8
sustaining Big Think
  Big Thinky Heads, 142–147
  difficulty of, 157–158
  promoting permanent change,
    139–140
SWOT (strengths, weaknesses,
    opportunities, and threats)
    analysis, 48

Tan, Chin Nam, 115
tapping into employees'
    dreams, 109–110
technology, forces of, 13
theater of the absurd, 141–142
thinking out-of-the-box, 16
Threadless.com, 57
Tide, 45
Toubia, Olivier, 63
Toyota, 35
transcendence strategy, 95–97
trend board, 32
Trojan horse, 2
  building, 23–24, 163
  developing and implementing
      idea, 14–15
  executing, 105–106
  fulfilling mission and, 119–120
  leadership and, 127–128
Turing, Alan, 125–126
Turing test, 125–126
Tyson, Mike, 105

Unilever, 9
Unilever Foods, 162
unternehmergeist, 150–153
The Use of Knowledge in
    Society (Hayek), 137

Virgin Atlantic Airways, 39
Virgin Galactic business plan,
    95

vision, 8
Vodafone, 39–40, 53–54
Volkswagen, 35, 56

Wagner, Richard, 62
Waiting for Godot (Beckett),
    141–142
Wales, Jimmy, 65, 137–138
Wal-Mart, 94
Wandering Moleskine Project,
    47
Weizenbaum, Joseph, 122
Welch, Jack, 17
Wells, H. G., 65
Weyler, Ralph, 116
Whole Foods, 7–8
  entrepreneurial spirit, 151–153
  essence strategy, 95
  natural food with emotional
      connection, 17
W Hotels, 39
Wikimedia Foundation, 65
Wikipedia, 65, 137–138
Williams-Sonoma, 34
word of mouth, 74
work/life balance, 148–149
work/play balance, 148–150

Yunus, Muhammad, 95, 144

Zara, 52, 89

About Schmitt

Bernd H. Schmitt is the Robert D. Calkins Professor of International Business at the Columbia Business School in New York.

Schmitt advises senior executives on strategy, creativity, and innovation. He has consulted for clients in B2C and B2B markets, including consumer package goods, automobile, electronics, software, financial services, pharmaceuticals, beauty and cosmetics, hospitality, telecommunications, media industries, and the arts. He is a frequent keynote speaker at conferences and corporate events worldwide.

Schmitt's previous books include *Experiential Marketing* and *Customer Experience Management,* among others. He has been profiled on CNNfn's "Business Unusual" show and in articles in business journals around the world. He has contributed articles on business issues to the *New York Times,* the *Asian Wall Street Journal,* and the *Financial Times.* He He has appeared on BBC, CNBC, CNBC-Asia, CNN, and NHK and on *"The Daily Show"* with Jon Stewart.

For additional Big Think cases, new tools, and information on Big Think events, please visit www.MeetSchmitt.com.